"*Teach Like a Queen* is an essential read for women in education, and for all school leaders who want to support their female colleagues to reach their potential. It's funny, insightful and all about empowering women. Who wouldn't want Michelle Obama in your classrooms?"

Vivienne Porritt OBE, Strategic Leader of WomenEd, Vice President of Chartered College of Education

"Cleverly using as its template a series of highly respected women in the public eye, this book offers powerful lessons for aspiring and current school leaders. From Jacinda Ardern to Michelle Obama, the inspiring lessons for leaders are wide-ranging and offer plenty of food for thought. Can you model the attitudes and attributes of these powerful women to give you the confidence and skills to pursue a leadership role? Can you put the lessons from the case studies into action to create change in your school? Read this book to find out how.

Teach Like a Queen offers a series of practical lessons for prospective school leaders, based around the life stories of a series of powerful and widely respected women. With case studies to show the application of the ideas on the ground, this book is full of practical strategies to help teachers secure and fulfil a leadership role. The book is a 'must read' for any teacher aspiring to school leadership and especially for female colleagues."

Sue Cowley, Author of over 30 books for teachers, including the international bestseller *Getting the Buggers to Behave*

Teach Like a Queen

Teach Like a Queen **explores teacher leadership like never before . . .**

This exciting and unique text brings together leadership theory, popular culture and action research to inspire and empower female teachers into leadership roles. *Teach Like a Queen* celebrates the successes of iconic women and translates their respective brilliance into becoming successful, dynamic and high-performing practitioners and educational leaders.

Focusing on seven key inspirational women as archetypes, the authors address emerging professional issues which will benefit classroom practitioners and leaders, each correlating to a different Nolan principle and inspirational queen. Inspired by the incredible work of WomenEd, including a Foreword from Vivienne Porritt, each lesson features:

▶ a constructed definition of each respective icon and how that translates into the teaching profession;

▶ a case study exploring how a female school leader experienced her own Queen moment and the leadership lesson it taught her;

▶ key lessons for aspiring leaders; and

▶ takeaway actions to channel your inner queen.

Illustrating how a diverse cross-section of women personify the leadership strength of their assigned principle in practice, *Teach Like a Queen* will empower female teachers to aspire to lead and equip them with practical strategies to secure and fulfil leadership roles.

Tracey Leese is an English and literacy specialist, senior leader, ECF Facilitator, parent governor and mother of two. Tracey is a proud feminist who is passionate about fighting for more recognition for women – especially in the workplace.

Christopher Barker is an esteemed mathematician, teacher and leader. Christopher is also an amateur performer in award-winning musical productions and fitness aficionado with a love of the arts and powerful women.

Teach Like a Queen

Lessons in Leadership from Great Contemporary Women

Tracey Leese and Christopher Barker
Illustrations by Lauren Brown

Routledge
Taylor & Francis Group
LONDON AND NEW YORK

Cover image: Lauren Brown

First published 2022
by Routledge
4 Park Square, Milton Park, Abingdon, Oxon OX14 4RN

and by Routledge
605 Third Avenue, New York, NY 10158

Routledge is an imprint of the Taylor & Francis Group, an informa business

© 2022 Tracey Leese and Christopher Barker

British Library Cataloguing-in-Publication Data
A catalogue record for this book is available from the British Library

Library of Congress Cataloging-in-Publication Data
Names: Leese, Tracey, author. | Barker, Christopher, author. | Brown,
    Lauren, illustrator.
Title: Teach like a queen : lessons in leadership from great contemporary
    women / Tracey Leese and Christopher Barker ; illustrations by Lauren
    Brown.
Description: First Edition. | New York : Routledge, 2022. | Includes
    bibliographical references and index. | Identifiers: LCCN 2021052564 |
    ISBN 9781032022314 (Hardback) | ISBN 9781032022321 (Paperback) |
    ISBN 9781003182474 (eBook)
Subjects: LCSH: Women school administrators. | Educational leadership. |
    Feminism and education. | School management and organization. |
    Women educators.
Classification: LCC LB2831.8 .L44 2022 | DDC 371.20082—dc23/eng/20220215
LC record available at https://lccn.loc.gov/2021052564

ISBN: 978-1-032-02231-4 (hbk)
ISBN: 978-1-032-02232-1 (pbk)
ISBN: 978-1-003-18247-4 (ebk)

DOI: 10.4324/9781003182474

Typeset in Optima
by Apex CoVantage, LLC

This book is dedicated to the memory of our ultimate queen . . .
our nanna Pamela Maddock.

Secondly, we'd like to dedicate *Teach Like a Queen* to the many queens
we've worked with and who have inspired us, some of whom have been kind enough
to contribute and assist with this project.

Finally, to the queens in teams, the queens with dreams, the queens behind
the scenes, the queens in harems and the queens who feel unseen – this is for you.

Contents

Acknowledgements — xi

About the Authors and Illustrator — xiii

Foreword by Vivienne Porritt OBE of WomenEd — xv

Preface: (The Ladies and) the Lake — xix

The Nolans in Principle and Practice — 1

1   Queen I and Openness: Michelle Obama — 9

2   Queen II and Honesty: RuPaul — 19

3   Queen III and Objectivity: Meghan Markle — 29

4   Queen IV and Selflessness: Lady Gaga — 39

5   Queen V and Integrity: Jacinda Ardern — 49

6   Queen VI and Accountability: Kim Kardashian — 59

7   Queen VII and Leadership: Malala Yousafzai — 69

8   Happily Ever After — 79

Afterword — 83

Index — 87

Acknowledgements

First and foremost this project would not have been possible without the inspiration and subsequent support from WomenEd – whose amazing work we wouldn't have been aware of without Claire Carroll-Wright's own incredible leadership journey.

Vivienne Porritt has been absolutely instrumental in bringing this project to life, in writing an incredible foreword and by embodying the values advocated by WomenEd in her support of two unknowns with nothing more in common than shared values which we thankfully managed to convey within an initial email!

A huge thank you to the team at Taylor & Francis/Routledge, especially Annamarie Kino for believing in us and helping us to shape our initial idea into something altogether more meaningful and to Molly Selby for her expertise in bringing this to life.

To our case study contributors – Mrs C, Mrs F, Mrs D, Mrs P, Mrs W, Mrs K and Miss B – you are the true queens of this book and we thank you sincerely for sharing your wisdom and brilliance with us, so that we may share it with others.

Thanks also to Caroline Harvey for her leadership coaching which by now has extended way beyond the initial brief and serves as a living reminder of how far the impact of leadership can reach.

It would also be remiss not to mention Toby Marlow and Lucy Moss whose musical *Six* unknowingly inspired us and took us on a creative journey which has led us here!

We are also incredibly grateful for the endorsements provided by Vivienne Porritt and Sue Cowley – whose books were essential to us navigating the early years of our own careers.

A monumental thank you to Lauren Brown – our long-time friend and now creative collaborator – for her incredible visuals and illustrations which have become as important as the words we've written. Her designs have ultimately inspired us to aim high, raise our game and to be as dedicated as she is to making the world a better (and more aesthetically pleasing) place!

Finally, thank you to Andrew Leese for the critiques and editing assistance – and to Jack and Ollie, who have had to share Mummy with this project selflessly to enable it to come to life.

About the Authors and Illustrator

Tracey Leese BA (hons) MA PGCE is an assistant headteacher, literacy and English specialist, ECF facilitator, parent governor, leadership coach and feminist. Tracey lives with her two sons and fellow teacher husband in Staffordshire.

Christopher Barker BSC (hons) MA PGCE is an esteemed mathematician, teacher and leader. Christopher is also an amateur performer in award-winning musical productions and fitness aficionado with a love of the arts and powerful women.

Lauren Brown BA (hons) is a graphic designer, illustrator, marketing expert and mother of two who attended the University of Salford. Lauren currently works as an art director and is a true creative with a passion for all things aesthetic, including interior design.

All three grew up in the market town of Middlewich in Cheshire.

Foreword

As I write the foreword to *Teach Like a Queen*, I think back to the first message I received from the authors asking me what I thought of their idea for an education book that would celebrate women teachers and leaders. At first, I thought they were joking as I had been labelled as the queen of WomenEd at our fifth birthday party and I celebrated this by wearing my blow-up crown given to me one Christmas.

Once I realised they were serious, I was hooked. Of course, women in education should be seen as queens as we are all amazing. Tracey and Christopher's definition of a queen is a woman who rises by elevating others. The seven global strategic leaders of WomenEd know over 40,000 such women yet this is a drop in the ocean.

This book describes queens who are towering public figures and draws lessons from their life and achievements. I was delighted to see Michelle Obama and Jacinda Ardern included and these are probably my favourite two. As world leaders in a masculinised world, it is easy to see how they can inspire other women, especially when compared to some of the examples of male leadership throughout the global pandemic. RuPaul and Kim Kardashian weren't in my long list however: which public women would be in your list of queens and why?

Additionally, *Teach Like a Queen* also parallels these women, who are household names, with the quiet, hard, and challenging work undertaken by the real queens of this book, the women who teach and lead brilliantly in our schools. And the lessons we can learn from all these women are significant. We know that all teachers are leaders, and, it turns out, women are "badass powerhouses" who are rather good at leadership!

If women are great leaders, why do we need this book?

WomenEd is a global grassroots movement of 160 volunteer network leaders who are passionate to connect, support and empower women educators and leaders. In a feminised profession, women leaders are disproportionately represented at senior levels, with women from underrepresented groups facing more barriers. Such under-representation is reflected in a shocking gender pay gap which includes a motherhood penalty and a lack of flexible working practices which would support more women to remain as leaders. The voices of women are also more muted across the education sector,[1] which is why a mic is included in our logo. Alongside Tracey and Christopher, our agenda is to enable more women to achieve their ambitions in education.

To do this, women need to be prepared to disrupt the status quo, as Lady Gaga is described as doing in the Queen IV chapter of this book, and organisational leaders need to grasp the moral yardstick and draw on the values and principles that *Teach Like a Queen* celebrates. I came into education as I believed it to be an ethical, equitable profession. It turns out that women educators are not treated as fairly as I absolutely expected so our profession needs to hear the clarion call of these queens and engage in a discussion about values, ethics and equity with women leading this conversation.

I was shouting out loud when I read in this book that women need to re-claim leadership of education and "perhaps renegotiate some of the accompanying assumptions". I would love to see how Kim Kardashian would respond to an Ofsted inspection or Michelle Obama would deal with trusts that pay a chief executive officer £201 per pupil.[2] Michelle Obama is the beacon of ethical leadership and Mrs P must have been channelling her when she tackled the inequity of the gender pay gap in education in the Queen III chapter. This gap can be addressed as Mrs P highlights when she negotiated her pay and working pattern and I imagine her drawing on RuPaul by sashaying away from that discussion!

Jacinda Ardern is a leader who, in my view, is a human being first and a leader second. Why is this a singular case worthy of applause? Surely all leaders should be like this? She demonstrates that strength and compassion can and must exist together in leadership. And like Ginger Rogers, who did all the same dance moves as Fred Astaire but backwards and in heels, Ardern is a world leader who had a baby early in her first term of office, smiled while continuing to record a speech during an earthquake and "breastfed at the UN general assembly". She is doing leadership differently and women everywhere can see in her a reflection of their own value-driven approach and what it can achieve. It is time to change the narrative around women and leadership.

What can we all do to bring about this change? Malala is a wonderful example of the impact of an individual and their personal story. The authors describe this as a ripple effect and WomenEd works in a similar way in working with one woman at a time, one organisation at a time, one systemic barrier at a time, if needed, to lift women up so they can claim their rightful place at the leadership table.

The teaching profession has a significant majority of women, and it is in our children's best interests to inspire and support women to lead and to shape education. WomenEd want ours to be an equitable profession in which every woman can be 10 per cent braver and succeed and where school leaders and CEOs are brave by deliberately developing a more equitable, fair profession. We applaud the contribution of *Teach Like a Queen* to this agenda especially for highlighting the practices of the real queens who are paving the way for others to lead as women.

Imagine a future in which schools and education are led by more queens – Tracey and Christopher ask you to revel in this as, once you can see it, we can all achieve it.

Finally, *Teach Like a Queen* left me reflecting on these key messages:

▶ Always be true to yourself.

▶ Recognise and celebrate your own strengths.

▶ Take people with you and grow talent.

▶ Prioritise authenticity over conformity.

▶ Find people who will lift you up.

▶ Challenge the narrative that being a parent is at the expense of being a leader.

▶ We are all charged with addressing the injustice of the barriers faced by women who want to lead.

I know you will take away other significant messages and cause your own ripples. Our waves will make a difference for future women leaders and the young women and men we nurture and inspire.

Vivienne Porritt OBE
Co-Founder and Global Strategic Leader of WomenEd

Finally, the real queens say it better than I can . . .
Mrs C:
Always be true to yourself.

Mrs P:
Avoid apologetic language.

Mrs W:
Take people with you and grow talent.

Miss B:
Leadership is much less personal than we assume.

Notes

1   University World News (2019) Behind the Silence and Silencing of Academic Women. Available at www.universityworldnews.com/post.php?story=2019031407 1633193 (accessed 3 August 2021).

2   Schools Week (2021) The Emerging "Super League" of Academy Trust CEO Pay. Available at https://schoolsweek.co.uk/the-emerging-super-league-of-academy-trust-ceo-pay (accessed 3 August 2021).

(THE LADIES AND) THE LAKE:

This is the starting point, and the place where history intersects society and celebrity.

Some key questions this chapter will address:

Why are queens significant historically and culturally?

What can we learn from actual and figurative queens?

What on earth has this got to do with teaching?

What is the ripple effect?

Let's think of the leadership of education as a lake – a vast body of water of which only the surface is visible from above the ground. The smooth surface is analogous to the established status quo of school leadership in the UK – predominately by men, and a minority of women – the vast majority of whom are white British. So while the lake's surface appears to be even, this belies a rather murkier reality below.

If we are to bring about change in how schools are led (and by whom), we must first recognise that the role of the individual is key and that women in leadership generally only hold the power they're brave enough to request. As individuals we hold more power than we realise, but that power is amplified when it is part of a wider movement. This book is an attempt to contribute to the incredible work taking place in addressing this injustice by highlighting the strength of each of us and the potential impact we each have the power to make.

The idea of a ripple effect is neither not new nor unique to what we're trying to accomplish. In the Queen's Christmas day Speech broadcast in 1975,[1] Her Majesty the Queen spoke of the value of small steps which culminate in a far larger outcome – "A big stone can make waves, but even the smallest stone changes the pattern of water . . . the combined effect can be enormous." In this case it is the specific pattern of the patriarchal equilibrium that we're trying to disturb. There are certain conditions in which a pebble's impact will be optimum, its speed, the time of year its thrown, the weather – and we believe that the current changing attitudes towards women inherent in society facilitates the perfect storm in order for our pebbles to have greater impact than ever.

In many ways the ripple effect is a leap of faith, it's putting something out into the world in the hope that something else, something bigger, will happen as a result – familiar territory for teachers who don't always see evidence of impact immediately, yet continue to strive for better outcomes for students in the belief that change will follow. Taking our lead from *the* Queen, we would urge each of you to know the value of your pebble you throw and use it intentionally (more of this later).

The Ladies

It was while watching the magnificent musical *Six*, which shines a light on the lives of Henry VIII's wives that we realised just how much the impact of queens has been suppressed by a male-dominated history.[2] Take Henry's sixth spouse, Catherine Parr, for instance; an educated woman who could speak French, Italian, Spanish and Latin, she became the first English woman to publish a book, by mentoring and cultivating her step-daughter Elizabeth's academic interests, made colossal waves with her pebble.[3] To have her achievements reduced to "survived" in a reductive rhyme feels like an indignity. Incidentally, for a monarch who had such a preoccupation with producing a future king, it is a huge coup for feminists everywhere that ultimately Henry's biggest achievement was his daughter, Elizabeth I, who ruled magnificently for 44 years through England's Golden Age, thereby rescuing the Tudor dynasty from the scandal and controversy which had come to define her father's rule. The very definition of a queen slaying her way into history.

In truth, as far back as Queen Nefertiti (c.1370–1330 BC), queens have led and shaped society. Together with her husband the revered pharaoh Akhenaten they revolutionised organised religion and led Egypt into one of the most prosperous eras of the ancient age.[4] As an icon of female power and beauty, Nefertiti was breaking ground while western civilisation was still gestating.

Taking Queen Victoria as another example, during her reign she led Great Britain through a period of unprecedented prosperity and progress, strengthened the British empire and ultimately forged a foundation on which the concept of modern society is founded. Admittedly her stance on female suffrage does not make her a paragon of progressive enlightenment, but still – she made things happen.[5]

These days earning the title of queen is done not exclusively by being born into a certain family or by marrying a titled individual. Earning the title of queen comes from your personality, your successes, the way you treat people. A regal father or husband is not required; in fact a male is not necessary at all, which feels altogether more fitting! Queendom 1–0 Patriarchy. Inspirational women in any field can be thought of as queens; our personal definition of a queen is someone who rises by elevating others. Women who are intangibly powerful and exert influence over others. These same women eschew societal norms, achieve more than they're apparently entitled to, who fight for recognition. In short: those badass powerhouses who are impossible to ignore. So while you might not be vying for the title of Queen of Pop, the titles of Queen of PowerPoint, Queen of Pupil Premium and Queen of Extra-Curricular are very much up for grabs in your school – as are any particular niches you feel like you can make your Queendom.

In popular culture, the word queen has transcended its regal roots. The term queen is now used less to denote birth right and status, and more to indicate influence and power. More recently, the word queen has been re-appropriated by the drag community to mean a formidable female alter-ego. Dressing as the opposite sex is simply being in drag, but being a queen requires confidence, self-awareness, open-mindedness and quick-wit, qualities which resonate with the aims of this book. A drag queen might not be the first thing that comes to mind when you're looking for teaching inspiration but finding and developing a version of yourself that empowers you and others to achieve things you wouldn't ordinarily be able to will absolutely have an impact on your ability to teach and lead.

The Queen Bee archetype is also commonplace in teen comedies; the character to whom others look for guidance, the character whose approval is sought by their peers and who likely styles out crises of confidence with aplomb. Trade out the snide one-liners for some board pens and you've got the makings of an excellent practitioner! In a rapidly changing society in which the voices of women are getting so loud that it's absolutely impossible to ignore, the term queen has evolved into a moniker designed to uplift and empower women and thus is what we mean by teaching like a queen. The very different connotations carried by "sir" as opposed to "miss" are unwittingly indicative of the tacit gender hierarchy in schools, and therefore the title of queen seems far more fitting.

For the sake of contrast, let's consider what "teaching like a king" would entail. Despotism (Henry VIII)? Nepoticide (Richard I)? Or some good old-fashioned usurping of the heir apparent (Stephen)? Somehow this does not inspire the same level of greatness as the actual title we've chosen.

There is no doubt that teaching and leadership are inextricably linked – we are all leaders of learning – so much so that evidence of whole school impact is often a requirement of accessing the upper pay scale. So whether it's acknowledged by your job title or not, as a teacher you're already a leader. In throwing out this allegorical pebble we are excited to see the eventual ripple effect. By which we mean that if every reader is inspired to apply for a TLR (teaching and learning responsibility) role and support their colleagues in doing the same we would eventually see more women in leadership roles within the profession. Who can say where this ripple effect may end?

If we each made it our mission to empower the women we work with and continually push ourselves and progress in our careers, and create a culture in which women can unapologetically ascend and are empowered to challenge discrimination what would the collective impact be? How would this affect the women you work with? The girls you teach? And – just maybe – eventually on the profession as a whole? Over the course of this book, we hope to show you how to harness queen power, take it and use intentionally; and to inspire you to empower as many other women as possible – because as far as we're concerned, this is key to achieving parity within the leadership of education. So, prepare to learn the value of your pebble and then to propel it intentionally because you never know just how many waves it might make.

Notes

1 Elizabeth, II. (1975) Christmas Day Message. Available at www.youtube.com/watch?v=un5-u686gCl (accessed 19 August 2021).
2 Marlow, T. & Moss, T. (2017) *Six*. London: Playbill UK.

3   Wilson, D. (2019) Catherine Parr: The Truth about the Wife Who "Survived". *History Extra*, 10 July. Available at www.historyextra.com/period/tudor/katherine-parr-marriage-henry-viii-husbands-death-writing (accessed 3 November 2020).

4   Cooney, K. (2018) *When Women Ruled the World*. Washington, DC: National Geographic Society.

5   Baird, J. (2016) *Victoria the Queen: An Intimate Biography of the Woman who Ruled an Empire*. New York: Random House.

THE
NOLANS
IN
PRINCIPLE
AND
PRACTICE

Here is where we engage with some leadership theory in order to establish our position

(spoiler alert: it involves more women).

We'll also explore the Nolan principles as the foundations of ethical leadership and introduce our queens as archetypes along with a rationale for the inclusion of each.

DOI: 10.4324/9781003182474-1

At its core, teaching is fundamentally about investing in people. Year on year we take on a new cohort of students, believe in them, share our knowledge and skills and ultimately equip them with the confidence to rise to the myriad obstacles presented by society (or at least the next key stage). In many ways, teaching parallels leadership, which begs the question – why in a female-centric profession do we have so few female leaders?

Is it that we are societally more inclined to see men as leaders as opposed to women? Certainly, the definition of leadership has evolved greatly since Thomas Carlyle concluded that leaders have a fixed set of shared characteristics in the mid-1800s. His trait leadership theory postulated that leadership is essentially an inheritable characteristic: born leaders, literally.[1] As the subsequent research indicates there are many types of leaders and styles of leadership: autocratic, distributed, transformational. Styles of leadership are context-specific and interchangeable depending on specific circumstances. And ultimately leadership is a social process[2] and therefore, cannot be separated from the wider forces and assumptions prevalent within society.

There a great deal of brilliant empirical qualitative research into how people become effective leaders in existence, but to be honest with you – that is not what this book is . . . rather this is an unashamed celebration of powerful women and their accomplishments in the hope that by admiring their collective courage, talent and impact we can affect change in a profession which so desperately needs more women front and centre. Enter *Teach Like a Queen* seeking to contribute to the brilliant work already happening to in order to change the system from within.[3] And we're not going to labour too much over *why* women aren't leading, and more on what we can do about it.

The Nolan Principles

There are countless facets of leadership and many ways that leading has been quantified and branded over the years, in the case of this book we have focused on 7 key leadership behaviours, which isn't to say that this an exhaustive definition of leadership, because leadership is absolutely about influence, empathy and bringing about change – but it should also be driven by values. For the purpose of the book, the Nolan principles will serve as a moral framework. By placing each of our chosen queens into the context of a specific Nolan principle, we'll explore how these fit into educational leadership. These principles for public life were first set out by Lord Nolan in 1995 and are included in the Ministerial Code of Practice, and form the ethical basis for conduct (and therefore leadership) at all levels within the public sector.[4]

In 1995 Michael Patrick Nolan (1928–2007) was given the invidious task by then Prime Minister, John Major of developing a code of ethics in order to hold all elected officers to account. Nolan was the founding chairman of the Committee on Standards in

Public Life and the subsequent principles are his legacy.[5] So, though the Nolan principles were not created specifically for the teaching profession, they do provide us with a moral yardstick against which public officers can be held to account. Ultimately, Nolan concluded that the seven key areas of selflessness, integrity, objectivity, accountability, openness, honestly and leadership were the bedrock of public life. In spite of the radical societal changes which have taken place since 1995, these principles somehow still feel entirely relevant.

Ethical leadership is paramount. Widely speaking, the concept of leadership has been dogged with masculine connotations and ideals for too long, this book is written in the hope that women in teaching can step into their power and perhaps renegotiate some of the accompanying assumptions. Clearly, leading ethically is not specific to women, however if we are to revolutionise the way a publicly funded profession is led then surely integrity needs to be at the heart? Therefore, these principles have been chosen, and are offered as, a working definition of leadership. Not as mutually exclusive traits but as the sum of its parts, each principle overlapping with the other creating a glorious Venn diagram with transparently value-driven leadership at the centre.

The Queens

During the COVID-19 pandemic female leadership emerged as a key (and unexpected) strength when coordinating national responses[6]. Women like Jacinda Ardern and Angela Merkel have challenged widely held assumptions about what good leadership looks like as well as providing irrefutable empirical evidence of their own respective brilliance. Similarly, the role of female leadership within teaching is quietly undergoing its own revolution, thanks to the amazing work of organisations such as WomenEd, who inspired and supported the writing of this book.

The majority of teachers are women but this does not translate to the leadership of education, most prevalently at secondary headship level. According to the Future Leaders Trust, in 2015, 74 per cent of teachers are women yet only 65 per cent of head-teachers are women.[7] More recent data from the Department for Education shows that in 2020 the percentage of female teachers had risen to 75 per cent and that women comprised 67 per cent of headteachers,[8] so while change is clearly under way, there is still so much more to do.

Clearly, the profession needs more females in leadership roles, as well as cultivating a culture in which women are championed, celebrated and supported. More women are also desperately needed at decision-making and policy-creating level if we are to truly address the lack of female representation within educational leadership. Which is where our queens come into play; while exploring and commandeering some of their brilliance we hope to reclaim leadership as something which is rooted in empathy, values and compassion and is ultimately achievable for all. And we'll be taking inspiration from women, not from the remote archives of history, but who are living and breathing the change we want to be today – who are not notable through hereditary peerage but on merit.

Leadership is not a destination, it's a process and even those at the hierarchical pinnacle of their career still need to dedicate time to honing and exercising these skills. Teaching is a profession which offers fresh challenges and new frontiers to pioneer. In which case, surely school leadership can never be over-practised? So, even if you are already in a leadership position (or if you're looking to get the most out of your female staff) our queens have lessons to move practice forward in your school.

Without further ado, we present our principle cast of leading ladies and their respective lessons:

- ▶ *Michelle Obama* will illustrate how openness is an essential aspect of ascending with dignity.
- ▶ *RuPaul* will school us in the importance of honestly, especially when flattery would be preferable.
- ▶ *Meghan Markle* will enable us to discuss women's fundamental fear of disapproval and how to overcome this, especially in the face of criticism.
- ▶ *Lady Gaga's* selfless approach will enable us to explore the vital role that teachers have in addressing social injustice and that sometimes disturbing the status quo is the way to achieve this.
- ▶ *Jacinda Ardern* is an undeniable queen who will offer us lessons in humanity and integrity and generally winning at leadership by it not being about you.
- ▶ *Kim Kardashian* is an unlikely queen who will serve us masterclasses in how to succeed with metric and how accountability can be positive and loaded with possibility.
- ▶ *Malala Yousafzai* is our final queen whose work on educating girls within a context of oppression reminds us of the importance of championing other women as we too climb.

These (perhaps unlikely) queens have been chosen as inspirational successful women who will allow us to illustrate specific aspects of the Nolan principles in action. Many of whom are also mothers who manage the demands of family life alongside their careers. Some of the queens are divisive and evoke very strong feelings, but therein too lie leadership lessons.

Disclaimer: these women are intended to function as archetypes who have unwittingly given us leadership lessons in the pursuit of their goals, response to criticism and how they rise to the challenges of public life. Clearly, the thought of Lady Gaga turning up to cover an unplanned French lesson is as ludicrous as it is unlikely. We will, however, explore the lives and achievements of these queens and translate their own respective brilliance into tangible lessons in our queens' own words for teachers. Also – at the risk of stating the obvious – our queens are not affiliated with us or this project, they are just amazing women.

In addition to those chosen, there were many others we could have included. In truth, researching this book has shown us just how prevalent strong female leaders are in contemporary society and popular culture, though they may not be recognised as leaders as we tend to define leadership through a patriarchal lens, leading to unconscious bias which unwittingly marginalises the achievements of women.

Furthermore, it's also worth noting that women are not a homogeneous group, and therefore barriers to leadership and progression differ greatly. But with that said, in writing, the recurring themes were hard to ignore: confidence, resilience and integrity were all issues negotiated by our case studies – and actual – queens alike.

In many ways school leadership is not domain-specific and that therefore we can learn a great deal from women who aren't teachers – ethics, communication and trust are ubiquitous, and these so-called soft skills when combined with the precise knowledge of education systems, curricular, pedagogy, assessment and people is exactly where the magic happens. By which, we mean the tools required to raise standards in school – which is surely the goal of every school leader.

Before we begin, it should be distinctly understood that because the queens serve as archetypes, they are not mutually exclusive, that is to say that it would be entirely reductive to assume that you need to choose the persona you identify with most in order to channel the leadership lessons we have to offer. Rather think of the lessons and women as personas you can channel in specific contexts and circumstances. With that said, you are likely to encounter women who embody these archetypes within your careers, so each chapter concludes with a summary of the key traits allowing you to identify (and learn from) these women. To further contextualise this, we have aligned a case study with each queen to illustrate said lesson and principle using real-life leaders from the profession the true queens of this book.

The case study queens have all traversed leadership terrain which feels both universal and specific to women: the desire to work flexibly, lead empathetically and empower others are designed to bring the more abstract lessons from our global icons into sharper focus when considered in the context of the operational running of a school. The leaders hold diverse posts within a range of education providers and yet there is commonality between some of the obstacles and solutions, and they epitomise the Nolan principles in all their glory. Each leader case studied are first-rate examples of the value-driven leadership we're striving for and frankly without them this book would be little more than us fangirling over Michelle Obama. More than this, each leader used their pebble intentionally and have made waves accordingly.

We hope you enjoy the masterclasses and practical strategies provided by our queens and perhaps just revel in the majesty of powerful women while we're there. So, we will watch in awe as Meghan Markle rises above criticism, marvel at Michelle Obama's ethical ascent to First Lady and allow ourselves to imagine how Kim Kardashian would likely slay an Ofsted inspection. There are universal lessons to be learnt from the way in which Lady Gaga champions minorities and how RuPaul gives feedback; and it is our sincere hope that the accomplishments of these remarkable women will ignite the same desire in you to teach and lead like these queens.

Some questions to consider as we begin:

- ▶ What is your definition of leadership?
- ▶ Who would you identify as a successful leader? Why?
- ▶ Which skills do teachers have already that lend themselves to leadership roles?
- ▶ How do you feel when you're around an effective leader?
- ▶ What examples of value-led leadership have you encountered?

Notes

1   Cherry, K. (2016) What is the Trait Theory of Leadership, 9. Available at www.verywell.com/what-is-the-trait-theory-of-leadership-2795322 (accessed 10 August 2021).
2   Gallos, J. (2008) *Business Leadership*. San Francisco, CA: Jossey-Bass.
3   Cowley, S. (2019) 10% Braver; Feel the Fear and do it Anyway. In Porritt, V. & Featherstone, K. (eds), *10% Braver*. London: Sage, p. 23.
4   Committee on Standards in Public Life (1995) The Seven Principles of Public Life. Available at www.gov.uk/government/publications/the-7-principles-of-public-life (accessed 1 August 2021).
5   Roth, A. (2007) Lord Nolan. *The Guardian*, 26 January. Available at www.theguardian.com/news/2007/jan/26/guardianobituaries.obituaries (accessed 3 August 2021).
6   Henley, J. (2020) Female-Led Countries Handled Coronavirus Better, Study Suggests. The Guardian, 18 August. Available at www.theguardian.com/world/2020/aug/18/female-led-countries-handled-coronavirus-better-study-jacinda-ardern-angela-merkel (accessed 12 February 2021).

7   Future Leaders Trust (2015) 1700 Female Headteachers "Missing" from England's Schools. Available at www.future-leaders.org.uk/documents/62/1700_FEMALE_HEADS_MISSING_FROM_ENGLISH_SCHOOLS.pdf (accessed 21 August 2021).

8   Department for Education (2020) School Workforce in England. Available at https://explore-education-statistics.service.gov.uk/find-statistics/school-workforce-in-england (accessed 21 August 2021).

QUEEN I AND OPENNESS:

Michelle Obama:

[adjective] To stand up to the highest level of scrutiny without fault or flaw.

See also: powerhouse, dignity.

"I knew my performance management appraisal would go well, my data is completely Michelle Obama.."

DOI: 10.4324/9781003182474-2

All hail Mighty Michelle, queen of queens and ultimate shero! Who better to start our journey with than the powerhouse that is Mrs O? As an undeniable class act, Michelle Obama engenders so much about what is right about leadership; a star who burns so brightly that she almost eclipses that man she married. It's not just that Michelle Obama's narrative arc began in the working classes of the South Side of Chicago and ended up at the White House, it's the fact that she accomplished this entirely (and obviously) ethically.

As the wife of the 44th President of the United States of America, and the first ever First Lady of colour,[1] Michelle Obama's success is often characterised by many as the embodiment of the American dream. Though it would be all too easy to see her ascent as emblematic of progressive societal change and shifting attitudes towards race, class and tolerance, in truth she is just a woman who wanted to make an impact and to use her talent for wider social betterment. And though she is so much more than the colour of her skin, it's hard not to fangirl over MO without acknowledging her lineage as a proud African American.

Michelle LaVaughn Robinson was born in January 1964, also notable as the year in which the Civil Rights Act was passed, an event which perhaps foreshadowed her eventual destiny. As a little over a century and a half before her inauguration as First Lady, her paternal great-great grandfather had been born into slavery.[2] It is little wonder that legions of women are inspired by her story which feels less like social mobility and more like a socio-political revolution.

Michelle's incredible trajectory is undoubtedly inspirational. As the youngest child of Marian and Fraser C. Robinson III, and sister to Craig, she was a diligent student from the onset. Michelle attributes some of her trademark resilience and stoicism to seeing her father's tremendous work ethic and commitment to addressing inequality while simultaneously battling multiple sclerosis.[3] Following her education at a high school for gifted children she attended Princeton University and then Harvard Law School, initially practising at the law firm Sidley and Austin.[4] While working there she had an existential epiphany which resulted in her opting for a more altruistic role in the public sector which she instinctively felt would be more fulfilling and it's perhaps this particular move which best exemplifies Michelle Obama's specific brilliance. Her choice to eschew a lucrative and prestigious role in favour of a post inherently more philanthropic sets her apart as a leader who is so clearly not motivated by personal gain but by a palpable desire to address social injustice and create a lasting leadership legacy.

I think we can agree that Michelle's inkling that she could be of use in the public sector was correct. By this time she'd met a certain Mr Obama, which also turned out pretty well. Together brand Obama have reached the apex of power in the modern world and continue to contribute to the global political and cultural landscape.

The level of scrutiny that accompanies living in the White House is almost unimaginable. The pressure to be perfect, to live the values you're representing and to deliver the goods to the people of America is a tall order further magnified by the thinly veiled racial slurs and negative press from right-wing media outlets. Clearly, the level of fortitude and grace it would take to rise above and remain focused on your goals is nothing less than laudable. And yet, throughout the eight years of the Obama administration we saw just that. Arguably, it's impossible to fake this level of authenticity (and certainly impossible to fake unnoticed). MO is the real deal when it comes to ethical leadership . . . and we are HERE FOR IT!

Becoming More Michelle

Openness and transparency are absolute non-negotiables when it comes to teaching, and through the accomplishments and conduct of Mrs O, we will explore this essential concept on several levels. Whether it's making a difficult decision, taking a stand against injustice or allocating public funds, the profession demands transparency. The role of a teacher is a privileged one and the accompanying moral responsibility should never be underestimated; in some ways this could be considered as analogous to the public scrutiny experienced by the Obamas, (albeit probably with a little less Givenchy). So how has Michelle Obama succeeded in being a leader who is both credible and formidable, and how can you commandeer some of her approach to boost your own leadership capital?

Wherever you are in your leadership journey, there is always room to be more Obama enabling you to make a similar impact by making MO's MO your own.

Lesson 1: Lead by Example with Hope, Never Fear[5]

The first (and most fundamental) lesson we can draw from the success of Michelle Obama is that you cannot fake ethical leadership, there are no short cuts or life hacks, being authentically driven by values is ultimately the bedrock of brilliance. One simple way to demonstrate your personal authenticity is through leading by example. All adults in schools serve as role models – knowingly or otherwise. Teachers instinctively know that bringing out the best in our students involves modelling the values and behaviour we expect, and of course this is equally applicable to leading.

Of course, the best way to establish leadership credibility is first to deliver the goods in the classroom and model what you expect of others. It is therefore essential that leaders should never consider themselves too important to do what they expect of others. If history has taught us anything about how *not* to lead, it's that some people cannot be trusted with power. It's really that simple. Perhaps you know leaders who don't practise what they preach and don't uphold the standards they expect of others, or worse exploit their position to make the lives of those they line manage or influence unpleasant. If not in teaching, perhaps in the wider sphere of leadership. This type of "leadership" comes at a cost; the loss of credibility, resentment from others and above all, it's just not right. Leadership should always seek to elevate others à la Mich, and if it isn't, can it really be considered leadership at all?

Having high expectations of staff and holding them to account is fundamental in establishing and building up your team. An open-style of leadership also boosts staff wellbeing, through clear processes, reasonable deadlines to complete tasks and absolute transparency. All of which should allay stress as opposed to causing it. This type of leadership is not geared towards "catching staff out" but instead builds a culture of shared ownership and high standards – which are the foundations upon which shared greatness and excellence can be built.

The notion of leading without fear is an interesting one, we all know that the stakes are high in terms of teacher accountability, but imagine being part of a team which is motivated by what's possible rather than probable. Teams with higher levels of openness and transparency are more likely to engender a climate of psychological safety[6] in which members will take more risks, operate more creatively and generally perform at a higher level. Psychological safety occurs when team members trust each other and their leader(s), clearly openness is integral to achieving this.

Level up the psychological safety in your team by:

▶ Taking responsibility for your own mistakes and own your own fallibility.

▶ Demonstrably appreciating all initiatives and ideas – whether they are workable or not.

▶ Promoting professional curiosity and risk taking.

▶ Involving stakeholders in the making of key decisions.

▶ Acknowledging leadership as the privilege it is and acting accordingly.

Lesson 2: Find People Who Will Lift You Up[7]

Let's be very clear here: as a leader this is your job; you are *people*. Though you indeed need to be surrounded by others who will lift you up, your main function as a leader should always be to elevate others. We get the sense that through the ascent of the Obamas they were both acutely aware of what their success would mean to others, because representation is always a precursor to inclusivity. So as you step forwards and break new ground, know that the people you work with will pay attention and though your future success doesn't depend on them democratically re-electing you, their perception does matter, so how can you channel the Obamas and turn up as the very best version of yourself? And better still, enable others to do the same?

One of Michelle Obama's standout characteristics is her ability to forge meaningful connections with others, regardless of her relationship with them, or how seemingly fleeting the interaction. This is one of her many talents which made her so integral to her husband's election campaigns. Perhaps this is due to Michelle's evident sincerity when engaging with others, she really strives to pay attention to others and focuses in on the conversation. Therefore, when you're in a meeting, or a lesson or CPD or any other form of professional interaction, really be present – and let this be known! This behaviour requires little practice and virtually no talent. Simply by resisting the temptation to draft an email, mark or check your phone, this signals that you value the time and input of others. Staff typically welcome interaction with leaders, so be present enough to make those moments count.

There is no doubt that teachers are incredibly skilled superheroes who shape the world, but it would be naïve to think that leaders can single-handedly cope with the various and ever-changing demands of the job. However, teachers can sometimes be closed off to the support and wisdom of other staff in schools. Perhaps because we are too busy to contemplate that there might be a better way of doing what they're doing or perhaps because so much of time is spent being the most knowledgeable person in the room that it's an alien concept that someone else in the team might have a better way of handling a situation. Do not underestimate the need to be open to collaboration, input and support of others.

On the whole, teachers are incredibly empathetic and warm people (it's pretty much in the job description), and of course you can lead and be kind to others just as you would in the classroom. Being open with those you lead doesn't mean sharing confidential information unsolicited, it's more about taking others with you as you rise, and creating a culture whereby others are involved in key-decisions and are invested in a shared vision. For example, is it better to tell someone that their lesson wasn't up to scratch after an observation, or for them to have the tools to see this for themselves? In the same way that we would endeavour to empower our students to identify their own next steps, we can certainly seek to equip our colleagues with the same skills and autonomy. Thereby creating a transparent and open culture facilitated by emotional intelligence and interpersonal skills just like Mrs O.

Lesson 3: Step Out of Your Comfort Zone and Soar[8]

Teaching can sometimes feel like a hamster wheel of new initiatives, and sometimes new ideas are actually old ones repackaged and branded to us as innovative practice. Sometimes these moments are met with cynicism – though commonplace in the profession, this could distract from the students and distract from trying to raise standards.

Therefore, it's vital that as a leader you are seen to be at the forefront of current thinking and empirical research in terms of the profession, and more than this, you should empower the team you lead to do the same. Do not fear new ideas, get on board enough to know which ones will work for you, your context and school-priorities. Throughout their tenure, the Obamas were seen to embrace new ideas wholeheartedly as part of their deliberate attempt to lead *differently*. Whether that was allowing 50 girl scouts to sleep over on the south lawn or by facilitating hip-hop dance lessons, they have made deliberate attempts to get among the people they lead, endearing themselves by with their unapologetically human touch.[9] While inviting the year 5 team to sleep over in your garden may seem a bit much, embracing new ideas surely is not.

Throughout her life, Michelle has striven to forge her own path. Having been warned by her high school career adviser not to set her sights too high,[10] Ms Obama has made it her business (and legacy) to do just that. As a graduate of Princeton and later Harvard Law School, she has worked tirelessly to not to be seen as a minority, but as a leader and captain of her own destiny on her own terms. By unapologetically setting her sights high, and achieving her own personal greatness she unknowingly empowers others to do the same, howsoever lowly the starting point. None of these achievements would have been possible had she not been open to new ideas and new challenges.

The teaching profession is constantly evolving, its refusal to stand still is one of the many reasons why the job is so fulfilling. This means that there are frequent occasions where you are asked to change your practice. This might be to reflect a change to the curriculum, the exam board specification, a new school policy or to meet the needs of an individual student. It can often be a teacher's first instinct to resist change when it's presented; a lot of teachers and leaders interpret change as increased workload. In fairness, sometimes it does create increased short-term workload but the change is likely being introduced to improve student outcomes and so some organisation between you and your team will need to happen to lessen this workload burden.

While it's important to be open to change, we're not advocating mindlessly agreeing to every idea that's put your way. You may be able to identify faults or obstacles which are important to iron out to allow the proposed changes to be successful. If you raise your points objectively, with a view to helping to implement the changes then you shouldn't be perceived as simply a naysayer. When you're the one implementing change you'll need this kind of feedback as when you've been working so closely on something you can't always see the potential barriers yourself.

The role of First Lady is determined by marriage, yet Michelle Obama refused to be defined by her choice of spouse. Theirs is a partnership of equality with shared visions and values, and Michelle has been absolutely integral to the success of brand Obama. As an active participant in the erstwhile president's campaign and subsequent administration, this queen has trailblazed her own journey. Much more than a figure head, Mrs O has shaped policy and championed her own distinct causes, making an indelible imprint not just on the USA, but as only a wider global scale and will surely be remembered as one of the most significant female leaders in history.

Case Study

Mrs F is a mother of one and senior leader in a large three-form entry primary school in the southeast of England. The school has a higher proportion of pupils with special educational needs and disabilities (SEND) and Pupil Premium entitlement in comparison to the national average, and is part of a Multi-Academy Trust. Mrs F was tasked with strengthening provision for pupils with SEND upon joining the school, in doing so, she channelled her inner Michelle Obama to improve provision (and later outcomes) for pupils with SEND and make a stand for students who had previously not had a voice.

Mrs F's starting point for what later became a culture shift around provision was to baseline what the school currently offered. She was surprised to find that the mindset of the staff was that it was the sole responsibility of the SENCO (SEND co-ordinator) to meet the needs of pupils with SEND, and was seen as a bolt-on, rather than an integral aspect of everyone's professional responsibility, which was not only the vision of Mrs H, but is also referenced in the SEND Code of Practice (2015)[11] and is an explicit expectation of Ofsted, not to mention stipulated in the core teacher standards. Worse than this, the SEND provision did not meet statutory expectations, with Ofsted looming, Mrs F was aware that the stakes were high and the overall school judgement could be limited by the approach to SEND, but luckily like Mrs Obama, Mrs F was not afraid of a challenge. Especially when there is injustice to correct.

Thus, Mrs F took this as an opportunity to start her own small-scale-high-impact revolution to pioneer a better deal for her school's most vulnerable students. Using her mantra "Every school is a SEND school" she fought to raise the profile and voice of students with SEND and upskill staff to meet their needs and introduce processes to ensure their progress. Initially staff were reticent, comments like "this is the job of the SENCO" were not uncommon. However, through actively teaching and support staff on the journey, and demonstrating the value of perceived "extra" work and placing this into the context of student impact, Mrs F gradually saw staff gradually buy-in to her vision.

To reinforce her expectations (and driven by the desire to build a culture of transparency and openness around SEND), Mrs F further engaged with a range of stakeholders including parents, governors and used student voice to further develop transparent, ethical leadership, this secured further buy in from staff. Before long the obvious improvements for students were sufficient to convince staff that the "extra work" was worthwhile, ultimately creating a shared goals and collective ownership of the provision for pupils with SEND needs.

The outcome of Mrs F's mission was plain to see – not only did the staff ultimately buy-in, pupils with SEND's needs were met in a transparent way, plus Ofsted and the local authority acknowledged SEND as a clear strength of the school . . . To top it all Mrs F's leadership was rewarded by her appointment as SEND lead across the whole of the MAT, allowing her to make a difference to students with additional needs on a much bigger scale. Like Michelle Obama, Mrs F saw injustice and sought to rectify it with increased accountability, transparency and openness, perhaps not changing the whole world like MO, but certainly changing the world of the children in her care.

Commandeer MO's MO in your school by:

▶ Choosing your words and actions carefully.

▶ Forming alliances with like-minded leaders to amplify your impact.

▶ Demystifying the rubric of leadership by speaking plainly and deliberately.

▶ Using encounters with brilliant colleagues as an opportunity to raise your game.

Look out for the Michelle Obama archetype within your school, network or career, seek her out and watch how she:

▶ Is not afraid of scrutiny or inspection because she has nothing to hide.

▶ Is equally comfortable behind the scenes as she is centre stage, and is not intimidated by figures of authority.

▶ Is warm and puts people at ease effortlessly and is able to build meaningful professional relationships.

▶ Has the gravitas and credibility to take on big causes (and will likely succeed).

Final Thought

Working openly with clear lines of accountability paired with emotional intelligence just like Michelle is truly the way to win at leadership.

Notes

1 The White House (2021) First Families. Available at www.whitehouse.gov/about-the-white-house/first-families/michelle-obama (accessed 1 February 2021).

2 Obama, M. (2018) *Becoming*. New York: Crown.

3 Ibid.

4 Ibid.

5 Obama, M. (2017). Michelle Obama's Final First Lady Speech. BBC, 6 January. Available at www.bbc.co.uk/news/av/world-us-canada-38537308 (accessed 28 January 2021).

6 Edmondson, A. (1999). Psychological Safety and Learning and Learning Behaviour in Work Teams. *Administrative Science Quarterly* 44(2) (June 1999). Available at https://web.mit.edu/curhan/www/docs/Articles/15341_Readings/Group_Perfor mance/Edmondson%20Psychological%20safety.pdf (accessed 19 August 2021).

7 Moss, H. (2011). Michelle Obama Reveals the Dating Advice she Gives to First Daughters. *The Huffington Post*, 7 December. Available at www.huffingtonpost. co.uk/entry/michelle-obama-dating-first-daughters_n_883838 (accessed 1 February 2021).

8 Obama, M. (2016) Remarks by The First Lady, Nick Cannon and Seth Meyers in a Discussion with Howard University Students. The White House, 1 September. Available at https://obamawhitehouse.archives.gov/the-press-office/2016/09/01/remarks-first-lady-nick-cannon-and-seth-meyers-discussion-howard (accessed 5 February 2021).

9 Obama, *Becoming*.

10 Ibid., pp. 65–67.

11 Department for Education (2014) SEND code of practice: 0 to 25 years. Available at www.gov.uk/government/publications/send-code-of-practice-0-to-25 (accessed 12 February 2021).

QUEEN II AND HONESTY:

RuPaul

[adjective] Unapologetically truthful and frank especially when flattery is preferable

> "After 5 parental complaints, I had a conversation with my ECT which was very RuPaul in tone."

DOI: 10.4324/9781003182474-3

Fabulous, fierce and formidable, RuPaul has proven over her career that she is as influential as she is revered. From humble beginnings, Ru has emerged as one of the most recognisable figures on the planet, trailblazing her way into our collective cultural conscious and is widely considered to be the most commercially successful drag queen of all time. Given the obstacles faced by Ru owing to her colour, sexuality, the fact that they dress as a woman, it is genuinely astounding to think about her stratospheric rise.

Ru is known for being many things – an actor, a musician, an entrepreneur – but, above all else, she is a leader; where her heels tread, others follow. Having risen through the ranks of celebrity through the 1990s and 2000s, she now reigns supreme at the judging desk on *Drag Race*. Essentially a prolonged job interview and performance management packaged up as entertainment, *Drag Race* has developed into a TV juggernaut and is now recognised as the most-decorated reality competition series, with 39 Emmy nominations and 19 wins.[1] RuPaul has essentially constructed her own drag curriculum (and much like in a traditional curriculum, reading is fundamental); *Drag Race* positions RuPaul as headteacher next to an analogous Chair of Governors Michelle Visage as they decide on the most suitable candidate on surely the most flamboyant interview panel and field ever.

You may be surprised to learn that if RuPaul hadn't become a performer, she would like to become a teacher.[2] While not the most obvious analogy for the profession, there are a plethora of parallels between drag and teaching; not least of all the requirement to create a professional persona which may not reflect your own personal demeanour – Ru herself identifies as an introvert who is naturally reserved, though you wouldn't know this from how she performs. And within *Drag Race* there are further aspects which translate to teaching, the need to adapt to change, model excellence, the requirement to use encouragement to build confidence and respond to low-stake failure. But at its heart *Drag Race* is about using Ru's expertise to enable others to be the most successful and fulfilled version of themselves possible – and isn't that what teaching is actually all about?

As an uncompromising mentor, RuPaul excels at building the capacity of her contestants. Moreover, she is able to get the best out of people by simply telling the truth. As teachers we are bound by the core teacher standards to uphold decency and professionalism, and though Ru may not be the obvious choice as a moral compass, there is much we can learn from her refusal to give unwarranted praise. Perhaps like millions across the world, you have seen Ru deliver her post-runway critique on *Drag Race*, if so, you'll know that she exacts standards higher than her most voluminous hair and doesn't let the opinions of her fellow judges nor the tears of the hopeful contestant preclude her from giving an honest appraisal, though perhaps delivered with a touch more shade than one would expect at parents' evening!

Shantay You Stay (Honest)[3]

Your own demeanour and confidence will likely be responsible for how naturally you are able to be honest in difficult discussions but it's achievable for everyone. RuPaul could definitely not be accused of rose-tinting her constructive criticism; when it's a particularly harsh message that a contestant needs to hear, her sincerity comes across which reminds the recipient that the intention is to help them improve, not to embarrass or insult them. The exact same rationale is true in a school setting, no teacher or leader should be aiming to humiliate their pupil or colleague, the intention is to help them achieve better outcomes or improve as a practitioner. While such straight-talking may not be your default mode, there will definitely be points in your career where you will need to channel Mama Ru.

The importance of honestly permeates the profession, from the vital role we play within safeguarding to the onus placed on accurate self-evaluation within accountability frameworks. Clearly, we are not talking about pursuing a monolithic truth or about imposing a subjective view of the profession onto others, but more the vital role that truth and honesty play within ethical leadership.

Lesson 1: All Tea, No Shade[4]

For those of you who are unfamiliar "all tea, no shade", a phrase popularised by RuPaul's *Drag Race* which essentially means "I don't mean to offend you but here's the truth" though it's decidedly less catchy. Teachers often find themselves in positions where they need to be honest to pupils, parents, colleagues and sometimes the awkwardness of the situation can lead staff to neglect key information or say things in a way which is too rose-tinted for the actual message to be understood.

Howsoever challenging, in the long run, it is always better to be honest in the school setting as, invariably, being less than truthful has a habit of coming back to haunt you later in the academic year. For instance, at parents' evening in a conversation with overly zealous parents who feel their child should move up a set when you know that all of your assessment data suggests that they shouldn't, it can be difficult for a teacher to state explicitly that there is little chance of the student moving up a set, because the child simply isn't able enough. Of course, no parent wants to hear that, however, this honesty is always preferable to a phone call later in the year from the parents questioning why their child is staying in their current set. Perhaps worse would be the scenario where the teacher has not been honest about an underperforming student whose parents are then surprised later in the year when their child does not perform in their phonics screening/SATs/GCSEs/A levels, only by then it's too late to remedy and the child's next steps or life chances have been adversely affected. Clearly, while honesty might feel uncomfortable in the moment, it's always the correct and ethical way to lead.

As teachers progress in their career, the challenge can shift from being honest with students/parents to their staff. Just as in the above example, a scenario where a less-than-great lesson has been observed it's important that the line manager is honest with the teacher as the consequences (such as complaints from parents or disappointed students on results day) are usually harder to deal with than being up front in the first place. That's not say that you should delight in savagely critiquing a member of staff à la Ru in a catwalk debrief, but rather ensure that however you deliver your feedback you don't shy away from being completely truthful just to spare an ephemeral moment of awkwardness or discomfort.

Lesson 2: Excuses Are for Losers[5]

But let's say you're not trying to motivate a class, or support an ECT (early career teacher). What if you need to tackle flagrant underperformance or unprofessionalism? Knowing your audience is key. Like Ru, who can be incredibly compassionate, but still full-on fierce, you'll likely know where on your assertiveness spectrum you need to place yourself depending on which student/ member of staff you're talking to. And this works both ways because when someone renowned for their honesty (and sometimes bluntness), delivers you a compliment it somehow carries far more gravitas than someone who is far more liberal with their praise. And isn't it a brilliant feeling to know that it really is positivity and not just a platitude?

And why is the pursuit of completely open and transparent feedback so crucial in the profession? Because it leads to better outcomes. So, though appraising an ECT more favourably than their ability may boost their confidence in the short-term, it won't help them to reflect and develop their practice, and it certainly won't help their classes to progress. As mentioned already, you may not give feedback to each teacher in the same way and, equally, the way you feedback to them will likely change as they progress through their training also. The same is true when giving feedback to your students, knowing your audience is crucial in ensuring their progress. Different students, different classes, different year groups, different key stages will all need different approaches from you when teaching them and, crucially, when making sure your feedback is understood. While the positive professional narrative with classes is powerful (see Queen VI), this should not amount to allowing a class or member of staff to become deluded about their ability.

Another of Ru's admirable qualities is her lack of time for excuses: when underperformance is challenged it can be all too easy for the contestant/student/member of staff to look for excuses rather than accepting the feedback and learning from it. When this happens Ru has little tolerance and is not intimidated by an emotional response (which many teachers and leaders may be). Instead, she openly rejects the excuse and refocuses the conversation. Teachers hear excuses from students all the time; "I wasn't the only one talking", "I didn't have time to do my homework last night" despite having had a full week to complete it, "I don't get it" having done nothing for 30 minutes and not telling you. Getting used to seeing through excuses and refusing to accept them with students helps them to aim higher and helps to prepare you for any situations where you might need to do the same thing with staff. The culture of "no excuses" also helps to promote high ambitions for students; you don't accept being PP/ FSM as a reason for poor performance, you don't accept poor behaviour from a class just because they're not the top set, you don't accept "I don't know" from a student who you question in a lesson – your high expectations are important and so are the different ways you communicate and enforce them depending on the audience.

In this respect, knowing your team, your classes and their parents is paramount and, where possible, seek to become an expert in your own stakeholders. Blunt truth might be motivational dynamite to some, but could cause others to implode. However you tailor your message, do ensure that the recipient is clear about the truth of the issue, and what you're actually trying to say. You may find it beneficial to back up the outcomes of such conversations via email if you suspect that the other party hasn't fully understood the message, this is also a transparent way of recording key messages.

Lesson 3: Don't Be Afraid to Sashay Away[6]

Difficult conversations. The clue is in the title really, they're difficult. They are not supposed to be comfortable but they are an essential tool in the profession, not least of all when holding others to account. Luckily Ru offers us lots of tips to facilitate these moments with your weave intact. Perhaps unsurprisingly, the success of a difficult conversation hinges on both parties. There are times when you as the conversation instigator can present yourself with the confidence of Ru in the Werk Room, be fastidiously well-prepared with all of the relevant facts and hold the interest of the students in mind but the conversation still goes awry. Sometimes the other party is just not ready to hear what they need to hear and it's important to know that it's okay (and importantly how) to end a discussion when the issue is not yet resolved.

Prior to a challenging conversation, it is helpful to have some key phrases in your head as an exit strategy. A particularly difficult parent or colleague may steer the conversation around in circles if given the opportunity so it can be helpful to have some stock phrases up your sleeve to punctuate the conversation and signal to the recipient that the conversation is over (for now). Expressions such as "Is now a good time for us to pause and reflect?" are a helpful means of buying both parties vital cooling off time. Another effective strategy is to pose the question "and is that you?" For example, when a team member doesn't want to teach a difficult class, or a student wants to give up, it's useful to ask so that the other party has the chance to consider whether they really want to be defined by the task they're unwilling to do.

Similarly useful, is to prepare for difficult conversations, do your research in advance and have the answers to the questions you're about to ask. Not as means to humiliate or outsmart the other party, but so that you have some semblance of what to expect during the conversation, and to manage your own assumptions. It can also be beneficial to channel Ru and explicitly state the reason for the conversation and any concerns you have as openly possible. Try to empathise with the recipient and be considerate of their wellbeing, make sure you listen to their points of view and really try to hear them. Where there are issues of underperformance it can be helpful to put your concerns in the context of student impact.

Finally, if despite your best efforts, the conversation escalates and feels more emotional than rational do not be afraid to end the conversation. Instead offer the other party the time and space to cool down and the opportunity to reschedule, perhaps with support from your line manager if appropriate, sashaying away accordingly in order to ensure that when the conversation can continue, it is professional and purposeful.

Relentless and determined (and did we mention fabulous?) Ru has her perfectly manicured fingers into many strategically placed pies. As a true agent of her own success, Ru serves as an example of how vision is nothing without dogged determination and that honesty is doubtlessly the best policy.

Other times you may need to sashay away:

▶ If you're working with leaders with opposing values.

▶ When being within your comfort zone is at the expense of your personal and professional growth.

▶ In order to broaden your horizons and allow you to experience other school contexts.

▶ When you're working beyond your current post and there isn't scope to renegotiate your job title or salary.

Case Study

Mrs K is an assistant headteacher within a specialist school who channelled her inner RuPaul during her time as a newly appointed SENCO. For context, the school in question had been placed in an Ofsted category ostensibly for its leadership and management but at the time of what follows, a new headteacher was in post. In the first term in role, Mrs K found herself in the invidious position of line managing her predecessor who had stepped down from the post of SENCO after bereavement to become a Teaching Assistant, it was in these circumstances that Mrs K learnt that honesty and integrity should be upheld at all costs.

SLT instructed that some highly disengaged boys should be removed from their lessons and absorbed by SEND to mitigate disruption from mainstream lessons. The directive included instructions that all 5 boys should achieve functional skills English and Maths, howsoever undeservedly. Notably, only one of the boys had an education, health and care plan (EHCP), the other was deemed SEN K (moderate learning difficulties), the other two were simply badly behaved and reached year 11 without seemingly ever being made accountable for their actions. It should also be understood that the nature of the functional qualifications at the time was rested on a coursework-type model with no examinations and a great deal of teacher judgement.

Mrs K had a reputation for succeeding with difficult students, and had always found a way to win over extremely hard-to-reach children. But this scenario was different, the boys had been told that they would "just pass" by Mrs K's SLT line manager and refused to even attempt learning. Mrs K was also mindful that this undermining disruption was happening under the watch of her predecessor who would have likely handled the situation differently.

The situation came to a head when not only had the students refused to complete any of the coursework for the qualifications, and had been rude to staff in the process (namely the teaching assistants line-managed by Mrs K). When Mrs K told the students that a failure to engage to would result in them failing the qualifications, the students dismissed this knowing of the SLT directive and an unofficial precedent whereby previous cohorts had been similarly disengaged but still managed to pass the qualifications. Mrs K found herself in a position where she either had to falsify data and appease her line manager in full view of the SEND team, or tell the truth and face the consequences, exactly as RuPaul would, she chose the latter.

Upon telling her line manager that there simply wasn't evidence for the students to pass, he was visibly unimpressed and urged her to reconsider. When she refused, Mrs K was instructed to present this at the next SLT meeting. Mrs K dutifully presented the behaviour data cross-referenced with students' work, attendance and "round robin" comments from the teaching assistants. Mrs K explained that any short-term gain on the school's figures caused by the students' achieving the grades would surely be countered with the message the boys would receive about accountability – and the likely effect this would have on their life chances and other grades. Mrs K was pleased to be supported by the headteacher who upheld her professional judgement and transparent leadership winning her legions of credibility with her team of teaching assistants.

Upon learning that they boys would have to actually have to work for their qualifications, they began to apply themselves and while very late in the game, two of them applied themselves and passed in earnest, while the other two joined (appropriate) level one college courses with far better attitudes as they knew that their eventual grades would be a genuine reflection of their engagement and effort and are currently in gainful employment. Mrs K credits the leadership opportunities which were later extended to her to this defining moment where she absolutely did not sashay away from the truth.

There will be a RuPaul archetype in your school or network, seek her out and note how:

▶ Her praise or endorsement carries huge gravitas among colleagues and students alike.

▶ She is a prolific talent-spotter and mentor.

▶ When she speaks people truly listen, and often she is the person others are trying to impress.

▶ She is genuine and authentic in all contexts.

Be more Ru in your school by:

▶ Striving for excellence in every aspect of your practice.

▶ Expecting excellence from others, and giving them feedback which enables them to achieve this.

▶ Knowing when to take yourself seriously, and when self-deprecation is key.

▶ Accepting that your power lies in the success of others.

Final Thought

Adopting Ru's "no excuses" approach to pursuing excellence and deploying honesty not as a weapon but as a tool to facilitate greatness is the hallmark of powerful leadership.

Notes

1   Nofl, J. (2021) RuPaul Just Werked His Way into the Guinness World Records. Available at https://ew.com/tv/rupaul-guinness-world-records (accessed 25 August 2021).

2   Vanity Fair (2019) RuPaul Answers Increasingly Personal Questions. YouTube, 20 November. Available at www.youtube.com/watch?v=72AAlCa1Nko (accessed 18 August 2021).

3   Borge, J. (2015) Decoding RuPaul's Drag Race: 16 Terms You Need to Know. *Marie Claire*, 4 March (online) Available at www.buzzfeed.com/erinlarosa/the-22-most-important-life-lessons-from-rupauls-drag-race Buzz Feed (accessed 25 August 2021).

4   Ibid.

5   La Rosa, E. (2013) The 22 Most Important Life Lessons from RuPaul's Drag Race. *Buzz Feed*, 4 March. Available at www.buzzfeed.com/erinlarosa/the-22-most-important-life-lessons-from-rupauls-drag-race (accessed 25 August 2021).

6   Borge, Decoding RuPaul's Drag Race.

QUEEN III AND OBJECTIVITY:

Meghan Markle

[verb] To demonstrate tenacity and resolve, refusing to take no for an answer, being unafraid to break new ground.

See also: trailblazer, pioneer.

"Reprographics said they couldn't laminate A3, so I meghan markled it."

DOI: 10.4324/9781003182474-4

Divisive and provocative, our repatriated duchess has absolutely perfected the art of polarising opinion – and her affiliation with the British monarchy, for better or worse, has shaken it to its very core. Born Rachel Meghan Markle in 1981 in Canoga Park, Los Angeles, Ms Markle perfectly illustrates the fundamental societal dichotomy faced by women, that is to say that she is expected to be intelligent but not intimidating, beautiful but not glamourous, vulnerable but not weak … Expectations which are surely as unattainable as they are paradoxical. No wonder she can't win.

After an initially idyllic and seamless integration into the firm, like Harry we were collectively smitten by her poise, her confidence and her charisma. Under the spell of the Markle Sparkle and after a honeymoon period which was both figurative and literal in nature, there was something of a shift in the way in which she was portrayed within the media. There were whispers of her being "ambitious" and "driven". Before long stories surfaced in which she was depicted as determined, assertive and direct (incidentally all terms which carry quite different connotations when applied to men).

It's fair to say that there's something of an established precedent whenever anyone marries into the monarchy; the outcome typically lands on one of two extreme ends of the spectrum of success. Many similarly potent and luminous women before Meghan tried (and failed) to diminish their own light so as to not outshine the institution they serve. The British monarchy is unique in that some of the leading figures' job is simply not to upstage the person or persons more senior (perhaps the opposite of what we're aiming for in this book). For a woman like Meghan, this was never going to be easy. She didn't join the monarchy at entry level, she had already accrued an impressive bank of cultural capital, political activism and industry experience. She already had a platform and a voice and was using it intentionally. Ironically it was this exact skillset which made it both probable and impossible for her transition from self-aware starlet to full time serving royal to prove as flawless as her wardrobe.

By 2019 the media rhetoric reached fever pitch when Meghan did not pose for photos immediately postpartum in full hair and make-up following the birth of her son, Archie, she and Harry did not share the names of his godparents nor allow the same press access compared to other senior royals. The media insisted that Meghan wanted the status afforded by her role within the royal family, but wasn't providing the requisite cooperation they expected. Either way, the media seemed determined to find fault with her every move, howsoever innocuous. It's a maxim mooted in reference to the monarchy to "never complain and never explain" But Meghan didn't have a still upper lip, nor the immovable British sensibility to suffer in silence. At this point, Meghan could have continued to try to appease the media, or to focus on the causes that matter to her, her family and her mental health. We all know which option she chose.

In January 2020 Harry and Meghan announced that they would no longer be based in the UK nor work as full-time royals. This news was met with shock and divided the nation. A series of events followed – interviews, a birth and commercial deals. In and among this, Meghan has emerged as something of a target for criticism, and it's her response to this with which this chapter is mostly concerned. And whether you are a fan of the duchess formerly known as HRH's actions or not there are clearly lessons we can take from her tenacity and ability to withstand criticism into our own leadership posts.

Objectivity Suits Your Goals

The need for objectivity within teaching is constant – it is a profession of high-stake accountability, the most significant of which being the impact we have on the life chances of young people. The concept of objectivity is far broader than simply being sufficiently detached from a situation to see it accurately, it's about resilience and knowing how and when to detach yourself so that your wellbeing does not pay the price of your (doubtless) dedication. The trouble is, that teaching is an inherently human(e) profession – one that is founded on relationships, emotional investment and (above all) caring. So, what does it mean to be truly objective within a profession which demands so much of our hearts and souls? How can we learn from Meghan to value and trust ourselves enough to fulfil the expectations necessitated by ethical leadership?

Lesson 1: Flattery and Criticism Go Down the Same Drain[1]

Taylor Swift may have had a point when she sang that "haters gonna hate"[2] because, do you know what? They might. Certainly, this is something to which Meghan – who has received the invidious accolade of being the most trolled individual ever – could attest. Many women are concerned about appearing as aggressive[3] and let this stop them from applying for leadership posts. What is perceived as "teacher bashing" in the media is also cited by teachers who leave the profession in the first few years as one of the factors.[4] The way in which teachers are viewed by others is evidently important and choosing comfort zones over promotion is one way to avoid feedback; clearly there is plenty to be gained from channelling Meghan.

Courting staff approval is both futile and foolish … and not a trait associated with trailblazing leadership. However, as teachers we are known for our resilience – something we have perfected in the classroom. Critiques from students can come to us in a variety of guises; a complaint from a parent, a snide remark written in an exercise book or on a test paper or perhaps the student may just overtly tell you. These annoyances are always going to crop up in teaching irrespective of how long it took you to plan your lesson, how many years of experience you have, or how relaxed or strict your approach with the students. While this aspect of the job is pretty much a constant, your response to it can vary: you could allow it to preoccupy yourself for the remainder of the day/week/term or you can rise above it, handle it in a professional manner and remind yourself that it's them not you.

As you step into a leadership role, the exact same mindset is needed. Just as with students, staff will give their leaders feedback – knowingly or otherwise. Step into leadership in the knowledge that staff will vent. This is a normal, even healthy, aspect of the profession. In the same way you wouldn't let negative student feedback govern your response to them, the same can be said in relation to staff. However, awareness of said feedback can work to your advantage: whenever making any decision which will impact staff pre-empt the feedback from the most negative, disengaged member of your team (in the same way that you'd plan a lesson which would hopefully engage your least motivated student). This often leads to identifying flaws and, crucially, remedying them before said member of staff delights in pointing this out during a whole-staff briefing. As long as you are principally basing your decisions on pupils' needs then this will lead to better outcomes for all as well as boosting your overall credibility – something which is far more valuable as a leader than approval.

Also, beware the "popular leader" as you perhaps would the "popular teacher" – which may be a result of low expectations and poor accountability. That's not to say that leaders can't be liked, but it isn't always the same as being respected. And should you receive negative feedback regardless, remember it's not personal in the same way you wouldn't take it personally if one of your students didn't work hard in your lesson. Like Meghan you can choose to tune this out, knowing that if your decisions are transparent, made with integrity and led by pupil need, you're probably doing the right thing – making this explicitly clear to those you lead is another key aspect of sound leadership within teaching. Clearly, objective leadership does not mean that you are impervious to criticism, but that you are not governed by it, and have the self-awareness and strategic overview to know when it is founded.

Like Meghan, you may find that some people are simply not winnable. Maybe because of someone who led them previously, maybe because of a previous school, maybe because of their personal circumstances and you may find that however hard you try or howsoever much you invest they simply do not respond. You will likely know these staff – these are the ones who you could give an extra free period to, and they'd question why they haven't had more. In this case invest your time and energy into securing the buy-in of the critical mass of your team and if the haters don't go with them, they will be in the minority and conspicuous for it. We're in it for the students and their outcomes and needs should always be prioritised over appeasing the mood Hoovers.

Put a pin in people pleasing by:

▶   Putting the rationale of big decisions into the context of student impact

▶ Referring to yourself using your job title when needed "As Foundation Stage lead, my preference would be …"

▶ Remembering that resistance to leadership is seldom about the leader

Lesson 2: It's about Boundaries and it's about Respect[5]

A key aspect of objectivity is to know and value yourself and your own boundaries, and to model this to your team. While teachers are known to be resilient, teaching with resilience is often mistakenly thought to be accepting every single task expected of you until you buckaroo yourself into oblivion. Like Meghan, having clear boundaries and expectations are essential in order to perform at a high standard in education. It can feel uncomfortable or unusual to say no when asked by your year 11s if you are able to put on an extra revision lesson for them or asked by your line manager to coach a member of staff from another department; your week, though your week is already likely to be saturated and so you really need to think through whether you actually have time. It's entirely futile to do several tasks poorly because you're overworked when you could do fewer tasks to a good standard, especially with the likely cost to your own wellbeing. No senior leader should ever respect you less for asking for a deadline to be extended, or for delegating an aspect of a task when your modus operandi is to perform and lead to a high standard. Meghan knew her worth enough to know how much of herself she was willing to give to her role. This isn't a lack of resilience but rather a process of preservation which in turns fosters even more resilience.

It's also worth remembering that the nature of the profession is that it will take up as much time as you allow. So if you have a week to complete your exams analysis document, the chances are it will take the full week – in the same way that if you had allocated yourself three hours it would still likely be done. Prioritise the time-sensitive parts of your role and allocate a realistic time in which to complete them and stick to it. More than this, promote this way of working to those you lead and influence, do not reward looking busy or staying late needlessly. Because, while your line manager is unlikely to think less of you for having a deadline extended as mentioned above, there are times where a deadline can't be extended and, obviously, Plan A is always to meet the deadline in the first place.

In teaching both time and resources are incredibly scarce and giving up and providing both readily is key for schools in all contexts … but that doesn't mean you have to simultaneously run a residential, attend the PTFA, run the school disco, and volunteer for cover all in the same day. And if you did, would you be considered more effective? More valued? More successful? Or would you just burn out?

In renegotiating her role as a senior member of the royal family, Meghan did the unthinkable: she asked for something which hadn't been asked for before. She had the vision and courage to imagine a different role in which she had more autonomy and presumably overall better wellbeing. Obviously, we're not advocating that you abdicate from the profession, but if you want to renegotiate your salary, the hours you work or if the demands your role and remit places on you should feel empowered to at least ask, and Meghan certainly offers us an excellent model of how this can be executed and how the distance afforded by an objective viewpoint is beneficial.

Lesson 3: Draw Your Own Box[6]

Another key aspect of objectivity is cultivating your own authenticity. Without question, we know what Meghan stands for, the causes she champions, the things she believes in. Being true to yourself is absolutely vital in establishing yourself as a worthy teacher and leader. It's also true that often some aspects of your role may require you to deliver a vision which is determined by forces beyond your control. It can be difficult to reconcile this with your own personal authenticity, knowing what you stand for and working in a school which is led by similarly authentic leaders with integrity should mean that you should be privy to the wider strategic vision and at the very least arm you with answers to the very questions others may ask of you. For instance, if a disgruntled student asked you your opinion on a detention they were issued you'd likely defend the teacher explaining the behaviour policy and the likely reason why they were given the detention, even if you wouldn't have necessarily dealt with the behaviour in the same way. In the same way, a member of your team might question the decisions of another leader in school and understanding that shared vision should allow you to explain the rationale for the choices made regardless of your personal opinions on them.

So, if being objectively authentic means being vulnerable to criticism, so be it. If being authentic means feeling so passionately about a cause results in you expressing an emotion, so be it. If being authentic involves treating others as humans and not as subordinates, so be it. If we all challenge some of the assumptions widely held about leadership more women are going to be inspired and empowered to step up. You may find that you're too luminous for some contexts, shine brightly anyway. And really, what's the alternative?

However, a word of caution here – you can't possibly care authentically and deeply about every single issue the profession will provide. Many royal watchers have questioned the wisdom of Meghan and Harry's decision to sue a tabloid newspaper and give a massive interview to Oprah, given that the response to this generated the very intrusion their change in roles has sought to avoid. So, by all means fight for the causes you truly care about, but do so knowing the likely cost and implications. Developing the oversight to know which causes really and truly matter, and the objectivity to know whether this is something of paramount importance to you or the students is key to creating meaningful impact.

As an absolute trailblazer whose presence and absence have been felt in equal measure, Meghan has pioneered her own role so that it works for her and her family, restoring and preserving both her mental health and her marriage. By refusing to accept the constraints of the role, knowing that this would inevitably result in further criticism, making decisions in line with her own beliefs and ideals regardless not only shows the extent of her tenacity, but also her integrity. We have had many women blend into the royal family before but we have never had another Meghan Markle.

Case Study

Mrs P is a mother of two and assistant curriculum leader who experienced her own Meghan Markle moments following the birth of her first son. While on maternity leave she decided that it would be better for her family and wellbeing for her to work part-time. The constraints on the timetable in this very small secondary school meant that flexible working opportunities were extremely limited and certainly not previously conducive for TLR holders, there was a precedent of staff typically choosing between the two (though this wasn't necessarily an official mandate).

Armed with the objective knowledge (and necessary data to substantiate this) that she made a sustained and valued contribution to the school, Mrs P was emboldened to try to bring about some change. Other staff members warned her against it, and were concerned that Mrs P would damage her credibility and relationship with the head – noting that the unwritten and unspoken code of the school meant that her request wouldn't even be considered.

However, empowered by a speech from then-Education Secretary Justine Greening about flexible working and staff retention[7] and (the magic word) wellbeing she set up a meeting with the headteacher to discuss her role and options. To Mrs P's surprise her headteacher was far more flexible than the staff narrative suggested. The head acknowledged that while the school doubtlessly would have preferred her to be in every day, having a teacher and leader as brilliant as Mrs P in school for fewer days was better than none! Better than that, Mrs P needn't choose between her leadership role and working flexibly. Unwittingly setting a precedent with the seemingly effortless way in which Mrs P appeared to have achieved this, and thus a new, altogether more flexible, staff culture was birthed (along with a number of actual births which followed).

When she later returned to work, she was greeted by the happy news that her Subject Leader was expecting, it was assumed that Mrs P would run the department during the Curriculum Leaders' imminent maternity leave. The unspoken precedent within the school was that historically Assistant Curriculum Leaders would deputise for Subject

Leaders short-term unpaid. Once again, she channelled Meghan Markle and asked to be paid for the role. While obviously an entirely reasonable request, in the context of an underfunded, leanly ran school this was an unheard of ask, deemed sufficiently enormous to present to governors. The request was granted and Mrs P went on to lead the department, paid and part-time. Possibly a minor Meghan moment to many, but utterly seismic in the life and career of Mrs P.

Bring some of the Markle Sparkle to your school by:

▶ Not defining yourself in relation to the criticism or validation of others.

▶ Showing your strength to your colleagues and students, if you must doubt yourself, do it privately.

▶ Asking for the things that no one else has – you never know what the outcome will be.

▶ Prioritising the projects which demand your emotional energy – budget your investment accordingly.

There will be a Meghan Markle archetype in every school or network. Watch her in action and see how she:

▶ Recovers from failure quickly or even flawlessly.

▶ Contributes to the school in a measured manner, very little is improvised nor impulsive.

▶ Is succeeding intentionally, her achievements are not accidental.

▶ Does not seek validation from others and may appear aloof because she isn't reliant on allies.

Final Thought

Being objective about yourself à la Meghan fosters resilience and enables you to live your best work life.

Notes

1   Liu, J. (2020) Meghan Markle Lives by the Quote to Tune Out Naysayers. CNBC, 29 September. Available at www.cnbc.com/2020/09/29/meghan-markle-lives-by-this-quote-to-tune-out-naysayers-stay-focused.html (accessed 1 November 2020).

2   Swift, T. (2014) Shake it Off. Los Angeles: Big Machine

3   Elias, E. (2018) Lessons Learned from Women in Leadership Positions. Available at https://content.iospress.com/articles/work/wor2675 (accessed 6 January 2021).

4   Weale, S. (2021) One in Three Teachers Plan to Quit, Says National Education Union Survey. *The Guardian*, 8 April. Available at www.theguardian.com/uk-news/2021/apr/08/one-in-three-uk-teachers-plan-to-quit-says-national-education-union-survey (accessed 1 December 2020).

5   Nicola, E. (2021) Meghan Markle Tells Oprah Everyone Should have a Right to Privacy. *Oprah Daily*, 9 March. Available at www.oprahdaily.com/entertainment/a35773234/meghan-markle-oprah-privacy-tabloids-exclusive-clip (accessed 5 May 2021).

6   Saylers, L. (2017). Why Meghan's "Draw Your Own Box" is Important beyond Race. *Forbes*, 2 December. Available at www.forbes.com/sites/lancesalyers/2017/12/02/why-meghan-markles-draw-your-own-box-is-important-beyond-race/?sh=3652a34c790d (accessed 4 January 2021).

7   Greening, J. (2017) New Support for Flexible Working in Schools Pledged at Submit. DfE, 30 October. Available at www.gov.uk/government/news/new-support-for-flexible-working-in-schools-pledged-at-summit (accessed 1 December 2020).

QUEEN IV
AND
SELFLESSNESS:

Lady Gaga:

[adjective] To act as advocate or champion for others, to make a stand against social injustice.

See also: altruist, philanthropist.

" I am not going to accept low aspirations from my disadvantaged students, instead I will make my seating plan more Lady Gaga. "

DOI: 10.4324/9781003182474-5

Don't be a drag, just be a queen:[1] salient advice that has boomed across dancefloors across the globe and inspired millions. Gaga's influence since her 2008 launch cannot be underestimated; helping to define the musical landscape for the decade ahead as well as educating her peers in how to cultivate a devoted, symbiotic fanbase. As both the architect of her own success and a self-aware arbiter of celebrity she is something of a paradox . . . self-assured yet humble, attention-seeking yet private, timeless yet contemporary. As a surreal caricature and master of her own iconography, LG may be a PR dream, but her talent is far more substantial than the gimmicks that first got our attention, Gaga has the depth, talent and credibility to achieve real longevity in an industry that thrives on fleeting and disposable success.

Born Stefani Joanne Angelina Germanotta in New York City in 1986, Gaga took up piano aged 4 and never looked back.[2] From the off she was dreaming big. The manner in which Lady Gaga commanded attention with her debut was nothing short of spectacular: she insisted that the public should anticipate big things from her and she has delivered the goods ever since. Her initial incarnation was constructed, potent and hard to ignore, the perfect off-the-shelf celebrity product ripe for public consumption. The evolution of Lady Gaga has subsequently and slowly peeled away the smoke, mirrors and subterfuge to reveal an authentic artist who's unique because in truth, she actually has more talent than fame. Her career has both exceeded and subverted the expectations of her fans and critics which continues to grip the globe's attention.

Gaga has always had a complicated relationship with the media, never more so than at the beginning of her career. Gaga's refusal to conform and the confidence with which she assaulted the zeitgeist disrupted a decade where members of the media treated female celebrities horrifically and largely did so unchallenged. The rumour mill responded to this self-assuredness by alleging that she was a hermaphrodite; that a male appendage was the only logical reason someone could be so secure in their own ability. Her deadpan reaction to this serves as an *étude* to teachers everywhere in how to quash a ridiculous comment from a student which has the potential to derail a lesson. She didn't refute it and essentially asked "so what if I am?" leaving interviewers looking like chumps and Gaga looking like a PR genius. Sensational.

Reign on Me[3]

While we could fill pages with Gaga's colossal talents and proportional successes in music, acting, art and fashion, it is the kindness that she exudes that we are particularly inspired by. Lady Gaga is not afraid to stand up for what she believes in and this often involves fighting to address injustices. Notably, she has actively supported the rights of the LGBTQ community and taken political stances when other popstars may shy away from doing so in case it alienates pockets of their fan base. She also used her platform to establish the Born This Way foundation which specifically promotes kindness and supports youth mental health[4]. More than merely support these causes, her selflessness and devotion to supporting people pervades her music and gives any individual (disenfranchised or not!) a feeling of belonging and that they are able to be themselves.

The teaching profession requires a Gaga-esque approach as we are essentially also advocates for minorities. Admittedly not the exact same minorities as LG, but minorities who need us nonetheless. Perhaps the most important role teachers have is to act as a champion for students who need it most . . . Arguably all students need this in order to succeed, but you will doubtlessly encounter students in your career who you'll know intuitively are more in need of this than others. Leaders and teachers have a vital role to play in addressing social injustice. Demographics such as students who qualify for Pupil Premium or those with SEND are helpful in holding teachers to account and as a means of addressing endemic inequality, but in truth there are other groups of students whose barriers to success might be harder to identify – mental illness, gender issues or those who simply struggle to be accepted, arguably these children are more likely to get overlooked if not part of a trackable demographic. So how can we can step into Gaga's (fabulous) shoes in order to become the advocate our students deserve? And how can we be both selfless and self-fulfilled in a profession which demands as much as teaching?

Lesson 1: Mother Monster[5]

In a world where you can be anything, they say, be kind. Better yet, achieve greatness and use that as a means of facilitating kindness on a bigger scale. Being a self-professed *Kindness Punk*,[6] selflessness is entwined with Lady Gaga's brand; she understands the influence that her position has and capitalises on this to make the world a kinder place. Her fans affectionately call her Mother Monster, a moniker which suggests she is a sort of pastoral leader for her many devotees. As the most (or one of the most) important adults in a student's life we have a duty to nurture them, to cultivate their minds and to ensure they feel safe at school. This is especially true for vulnerable groups of students as they may not have this same feeling at home and school is often the safest and most consistent environment students will encounter.

If all of the students you teach and all of the staff you work with conduct themselves perfectly then kindness is easy. Selflessness is required when being kind isn't easy: when a student has been consistently lazy and needs your help the day before an exam, when a member of staff who was rude to you last week now needs your help, when you offer a clean slate to the student who had to be removed from your last lesson. Teachers are humans and they are not immune from being aggravated by others and it can be hard to rise above a certain situation which has made you feel less than regal but it's important to remember that you are the adult or leader in the situation and it's important to model how to put your position before your ego and respond with kindness, especially with the least kind individuals you encounter.

Staff working in schools are often frantically busy; consequently, teachers and leaders find themselves firefighting, handling problems or issues that have arisen or responding to demands from higher echelons of the management structure. As a teacher who consistently acts in the best interests of the students, particularly those who are disaffected, it can feel as though recognition and praise is in short supply and this can be difficult to reconcile. This, unfortunately, is a likely part of the profession and you need to try to not allow this to demotivate you; instead, take heart in the knowledge that you've been putting the students' needs first – since the profession can sometimes feel inherently thankless.

With that said, as a teacher and leader, you are in the privileged position to create and contribute to a culture of kindness and praise. Praise is perhaps the most powerful tool in a teachers' arsenal, it can inspire, raise aspiration and ultimate facilitate greatness – and not just from your pupils. Praise for staff in schools often manifests itself as a bottle of wine at the end of the school year, or a box of biscuits in the staffroom – and while no one is likely to object to this, the fundamental lack of recognition in teaching surely calls for a more systematic and frequent approach. As a leader dedicate a part of your working week to celebrating your team this could be formalised like peer feedback as part of Performance Management or something relatively low-stake such as leaving a hand-written note on a colleague's desk. Deploy the exact same positive narrative techniques as you would with your students and take care to ensure that praise is used specifically and is well-earned. If being a school kindness punk seems a little too saccharine for you, consider it simply showing the staff you lead that they matter – something you have doubtlessly perfected in the classroom.

Lesson 2: Antithesis of the Status Quo[7]

One of the most exciting things about Lady Gaga is her absolute rejection of the status quo; she is constantly evolving and trying new things. While you might raise an eyebrow or two by rocking up to assembly in a meat dress (most probably from the textiles department), purposely bettering yourself at every opportunity will certainly help keep the job exciting and gives your students the best opportunities to be successful. As teachers, we can learn a great deal from the evolution of LG and her readiness to master every single project she encounters.

The education sector attracts individuals who love learning; we're passionate about knowledge, skills and passing this knowledge on to others. Despite this, the mention of continuing professional development (CPD) can be met with eye rolls and derision. Regardless of your thoughts on CPD, it's crucial that you refuse to stand still with your teaching; not least because you owe it to your students to be the best version of yourself possible to ensure their best possible outcomes.

It's entirely plausible that you may find yourself in training sessions where you feel like you're not learning something and your time would be better spent marking or planning. In this scenario you can either bemoan the fact to your colleagues and wind them up in the process or you can be more proactive and seek out your own development or offer to lead a training session next time; LG would likely choose the latter. CPD can sometimes be thought of as an externally run course (you know – the ones with the nice lunches and a few familiar faces), but in reality, sometimes the best CPD can be watching experts in action. Similarly, you can upskill yourself without rinsing the CPD budget. For example, online networks and forums provide lots of resources that can be used to improve your subject knowledge or pedagogy, other staff in your school will have knowledge and expertise to tap into, as well as your chance to observe some of your school's best practitioners in action just by you both doing your respective jobs.

This quest to keep learning and improve your practice (even if it's not at the scale of LG) is inherently selfless as it is a recognition that you want to deliver a better quality of education for the students in your school and until every single child in the school consistently makes good progress, there is still more to learn and more to improve on. This is of particular significance to groups of students who are predisposed to make less progress than others. As education practitioners we are very aware of the impact that quality first teaching has for disadvantaged students which is why it is so important that we carve out time to improve: whether your priority is your own teaching or you're in a position where you need to improve the outcomes for the students of your colleagues the pursuit of self-improvement is of the utmost importance.

Lesson 3: A Discipline for Passion[8]

Gaga has been vocal about her history of substance abuse, her mental illness and her physical health. She is an advocate for wellness in its broadest sense. In the same way, staff wellbeing is very much *en vogue* in the profession and as teachers and leaders we need to be aware of how to manage our own expectations and workloads in order to cope with the myriad demands of the profession. In order to create a culture in which staff wellness is a priority as with so many other aspects of leadership, you must model what you expect of others. It's also something we should seek to role-model to our students too.

One clear way you can model staff wellbeing is by openly talking about the measures you take to facilitate your own work–life balance – in communicating this to your team you are in effect giving them the permission to do the same. Secondly, set boundaries and do not be afraid to enforce them, again this will empower other staff to do the same. Of course, the demands of teaching are limitless and every task on your to do list could be considered important, but not every task will be equally urgent. Prioritise your tasks and if it can wait, let it. Wellbeing is a form of discipline in that it would be easy to work until midnight every night and live off caffeine and sugar during term-time, but this is not going to allow you to be the best leader or example to others.

It may seem strange to discuss staff well-being in the context of selflessness; however, if you fail to keep your own health in check then you will be render yourself unable to get the best outcomes from your students. Echoing thoughts from lesson 2, teachers and leaders need to be the best version of themself to get the best outcomes from their students. While we've already discussed the idea that this involves being as knowledgeable as possible and equipping yourself with the best skillset, it also means that you need to be well enough and mentally agile enough to cope with the demands of the career. A teacher who has worked themselves into the ground and is exhausted in front of their class simply will not elicit the same engagement and progress from a teacher who is well rested and energised, and it's definitely not how Gaga shows up.

Ultimately, the alter-ego of Stefani Joanne Angelina Germanotta is firmly established as a staple of twenty first-century popular culture, as a singer, songwriter, actress, activist producer and global icon her impact is undeniable. The lasting and indelible imprint she has already left on our collective consciousness is only the beginning of her eventual legacy. Doubtlessly, Gaga is an absolute polymath who's made altruism her signature move and thus a star (and subsequent other galaxies) was born.

Case Study

Mrs W is an assistant principal in a FE college, whose inner Gaga has championed vulnerable students within her institution. By boosting their life chances and fighting systemic discrimination selflessly, Mrs W was able to bring about a shared culture around the provision for students with Pupil Premium entitlement, where the needs of these students are at the forefront of the college's practice. Mrs W sees herself *in loco parentis* (read: "a nagging mum") on behalf of Pupil Premium students to ensure a bespoke person-centred approach in addressing endemic generational social disadvantage.

While meeting the needs of students in receipt of Pupil Premium has many strands, Mrs W cites holding middle leaders to account as integral to this, relentlessly questioning the setting, mentoring of tracking of Pupil Premium students and fighting to ensure that every single member of staff is held to account for the vital role they each play in addressing social injustice, all of which is *très* Gaga.

Mrs W sees her role as Pupil Premium lead as something which transcends school accountability measures, and unapologetically fights so that the school recognises each child as an individual with diverse needs and unique challenges. She prides herself as being a leader who compassionately challenges assumptions about student demographics, and as someone who instead responds to emerging student needs. The litmus test Mrs W has adopted is whether the intervention and provision offered to address disadvantage would be sufficient for her own children, and not stopping until she is satisfied that it is.

One such emerging issue concerned Pupil Premium year 12 students struggling to cope with the transition to key stage 5. More specifically the academic demands of level 3/A level courses, which had previously resulted in high course dropout rates, low attendance, poor engagement and disproportionately high levels of NEETs. In order to hone in on specific barriers to achievement for students in receipt of Pupil Premium, Mrs W initiated a 360 diagnostic, the student interviews which constituted this identified conventional academic obstacles such as low aspiration or poor organisation, but more holistic factors – many had never learnt to swim, eaten in a restaurant or visited a beach.

In response, Mrs W channelled Gaga by thinking outside of the box and together with other practitioners, introduced an accredited work-skills qualification, ostensibly to act as a supportive stepping stone to level 3 qualifications, but also as a means to secrete the cultural capital opportunities which had been previously lacking. Furthermore, Mrs W also used the qualification as an opportunity to invest in high-quality careers advice and guidance (CIAG) to further maximise the life-chances of the students.

Mrs W's selflessness paid off, since the launch of the programme NEETS have been eradicated, attendance has increased and destination data shows that more Pupil Premium students are now in Higher Education. This wasn't only selfless on an altruistic level, but also an example of selfless whole-school leadership, since the results of the qualification did not directly impact on the college's accountability data, it did, however develop the confidence, aspiration and ultimately the eventual lives of these students, and even though the data didn't count, those students certainly did, ultimately making the impact immeasurable.

Ways to make your everyday more Gaga:

▶ Prioritise authenticity over conformity.

▶ Eschew people pleasing in favour of asking difficult questions of others.

▶ Get out of your comfort zone frequently and publicly and without apology.

▶ Share and wear your talents openly even (and especially) if it intimidates others.

▶ Pursue wellbeing with the same fervour as you would academic results.

Look for the Lady Gaga archetype within your school/ network and note how:

▶ She is highly intuitive and has an affinity for the oppressed.

▶ She is perceived as bold and courageous because she does not fear confrontation, nor does she court approval generally.

▶ Her confidence can be misinterpreted as arrogance because she is aware that she is incredibly talented and does not pretend otherwise.

▶ She is a polymath and is likely to be accomplished in a number of fields.

Final Thought

Be more Gaga in your approach to disadvantage and wellness in its broadest sense, for staff as well as students.

Notes

1   Lady Gaga (2011). Born This Way. New York: Interscope.
2   Biography.com (2014) Lady Gaga Biography. Available at www.biography.com/ musician/lady-gaga#:~:text=Now%20known%20as%20Lady%20Gaga,Catho lic%20school%20in%20the%20city. (accessed 25 August 2021).
3   Lady Gaga and Ariana Grande (2020). Rain on Me. Los Angeles, CA: Interscope.
4   Born This Way Foundation (2021) Born This Way Foundation. Available at https:// bornthisway.foundation (accessed 25 August 2021).
5   Dicker, C. (2017). *Lady Gaga Biography: The "Mother Monster" of the Music Industry Revealed*. Digital Publishing Group.
6   Gordon, E. (2020) Lady Gaga Leads the Kindness Punks in a Fight for Peace in Stupid Love Video. Pop Dust, 28 February. Available at www.popdust.com/lady-gaga-stupid-love-2645329220.html (accessed 25 August 2021).

7   Yale University (2015, October 24) Emotion Revolution Closing Session. Available at www.youtube.com/watch?v=P5Xus-Y0biQ (accessed 18 August 2021).

8   Grant, S. (2019) Watch Lady Gaga's Shallow Oscar Speech: If You Have a Dream, Fight For It. *Rolling Stone*, 24 February. Available at www.rollingstone.com/movies/movie-news/lady-gaga-oscars-shallow-speech-799596 (accessed 25 August 2021).

QUEEN V
AND
INTEGRITY:

Jacinda Ardern

[Verb] To act with conviction and purpose, being led by the highest level of morality.

See also: goddess, principled.

"I noticed you didn't turn up for break duty, I am afraid I will have to Jacinda Ardern you to your line manager."

DOI: 10.4324/9781003182474-6

Oh Jacinda, Jacinda. How we love thee! Let us count the ways. This is not an entirely rhetorical statement since we are literally going to spend this chapter justifying the mass adoration Ms Ardern has garnered in her tenure as prime minister of New Zealand. With her unapologetically progressive and altruistic approach, Jacinda has reclaimed leadership, offering a humane, person-centred alternative to a leader-centric approach, showing that strength and kindness can coexist – and when it does the outcome is truly glorious.

Jacinda Ardern made history in October 2017 by becoming the youngest ever world global leader aged 37. Born in Hamilton, NZ in 1980, the second of two daughters. Her father was a police officer and her mother was a school catering assistant.[1] This very ordinary set up belies the extraordinary leadership journey ahead, and could possibly account for the warmth and humility which would come to characterise her approach. It was Jacinda's aunt, an established member of the NZ Labour party who recruited a teenaged Jacinda into politics and set our queen on course to prime ministerhood.

Now, while we don't define JA by the fact that she was only the second ever elected leader of modern times to give birth in office, can we just take a moment to fully register the level of magnificence this denotes? Upon making the announcement that she was expecting mere months into her first term of office, she unknowingly trailblazed the way for working women everywhere and stuck it to the patriarchy while she was at it. Not to mention the time she breastfed at the UN general assembly,[2] scoring a solid 500 out of 10 on the spectrum of queening.

So what is JA's secret power? How is it that she is universally loved? What's the magic bullet? Well . . . staggeringly it's this: She's. Really. Nice. Not just nice, someone who isn't afraid to show empathy or vulnerability, who's value-driven and refuses to slate others. Clearly this is beyond nice, this is integrity. And while Ms Ardern is educated, charismatic and articulate, this is the basis of her leadership – and the impact is irrefutable.

The idea of being a kind leader is a curious one. The trope of women playing nice is well rehearsed, women are hard-wired to nurture and therefore implicitly to please and therefore for women who lead the requirement to be "brave enough to risk disapproval"[3] is clear. And yet in Jacinda Ardern we have a leader who does not seek approval, but through sustained, meaningful and transparent leadership, receives it anyway. Clearly JA is not led by popularity yet by leading ethically and empathetically it would seem that universal approval is an incidental (but brilliant) by-product.

But it's even more than this, there is something in Jacinda's approach which seems like a conscious choice to politicise and lead differently. There is a real sense of her being led by values which transcend political affiliations. In the often morally murky, leader-centric landscape of world government Jacinda's approach of cohesion, authenticity and empathy has built up a sense of trust and safety which is so far removed from other world leaders, that it doesn't really feel like politics . . . in a really good way.

Integrity Has a New Zeal

The significance of integrity within schools is hard to overstate; and much of what we teach our pupils isn't from a lesson plan or scheme of learning but from how we behave and respond to others (see also Queen I, Michelle Obama). Integrity is also the foundation of value-driven, ethical leadership which in many ways is inextricable from the other queeny qualities we're exploring here, arguably integrity is a product of the actualisation of these other traits. The common thread connecting these ideas is professional trust; something required to instil and inspire in order to facilitate integrity. So, what does this look like in action? And how can we be more Ardern in our approach to bring about effective school leadership to enable better outcomes and experiences for our students?

Lesson 1: Be Both Compassionate and Strong[4]

One of the defining features of so-called Ardernism is her ability to unite others irrespective of differences. During the COVID-19 pandemic, Prime Minister Ardern's directive that MPs must take a 20 per cent pay cut[5] in solidarity with New Zealand workers who'd been adversely affected financially felt both simultaneously utterly radical and eminently sensible. This level of selfless humility sets Jacinda apart from other world leaders and epitomises her altruistic, humane approach.

It seems that whatever the issue, Jacinda Ardern finds the human angle and views it through a lens of compassion. For example, when British backpacker, Grace Millane was murdered she offered a sincere and emotional apology to her parents.[6] In seeing a diplomatic issue in inherently humane terms and responding with compassion where others might offer retribution, Jacinda further elevated her leadership onto a higher moral plane, something which we can totally commandeer for school leadership.

Teachers interact with so many people that it can be easy to forget that each of these separate people has their own worries, their own stresses, their own priorities. Any of these myriad individuals may need your help or influence as a teacher at any point; whether it's a new student lost in the corridor, a colleague exasperated about a particular lesson that went awry or a parent who wants to share a concern with you about their child. Whatever the scenario, that issue is likely to be a big deal in their life at that instant and being mindful of this helps to handle the situations with compassion. No one wants to feel like their issue is not important and feel dismissed by someone else.

Sometimes school accountability measures can result in leaders seeing children's attainment in terms of data or headline figures, instead of as the gateway to children's life chances. It is vital that in your teaching you harness your Ardernesque-strength and fight to ensure that children are not mistaken for statistics nor defined by a demographic to which they belong. The categories of SEND, Pupil Premium, most-able are there to ensure that students' needs are met and not to serve as a box to tick or to reinforce pervasive stereotypes – or worse – to justify underachievement. So however big your platform becomes it's important to fight so that student attainment in seen through the same compassionate lens used by JA and consider their achievements in context of individual students' lives, not just as reportable data.

Leading with compassion is not:

▶ Ignoring underperformance.

▶ Having low expectations of staff and students.

▶ Tolerating being deliberately undermined or disrespected.

▶ A lack of boundaries.

Lesson 2: Allow Positivity to Outweigh Negativity[7]

While teaching is a remarkably rewarding career, it is not without its annoyances; whether it's workload, poor behaviour or something else entirely, there's always likely to be a reason to vent. It's important, though, to make a conscious decision to dilute this negativity with the abundant positives that the job has to offer. Not only will this help to keep your own outlook rosy, it will undoubtedly have an effect on those around you too.

In the aftermath of the Christchurch terror attack, Ardern's response was humane and graceful: she refused to mention the perpetrator's name, refusing to grant infamy to the terrorist.[8] Once again showing us the power of emotional intelligence within leadership. Whist clearly, the issue of behaviour management is extremely far removed from terrorism, refusing to reward infamy is an effective means of managing behaviour. In your classroom you will likely have a culture where students receive specific praise in front of others, and you don't wish to draw attention to the serial-disrupter and so you respond firmly and discretely because the last thing children need is to associate negative behaviour with attention. Similarly, your school's Behaviour for Learning policy is likely to be reward-heavy and underpinned by sanctions which are far lower key, because just like Jacinda, we don't reward infamy. A nice strategy that can help to outweigh the negatives with student behaviour is to ensure that you end the day with positive phone calls home. This helps you to leave on a positive note as well as rewarding the students who have improved or are consistently doing well which can often be overlooked.

As you gain responsibility, it is an unfortunate but necessary reality that at some point you will need to tackle underperformance, the way in which this is approached is also an unwitting indication of your integrity, so caution is needed. In fact, the exact same approach you'd use in the classroom can be applied here to ensure that your Ardernism is on point. Therefore, it's essential that any issues of capability should be dealt with one-to-one and discussed only with that member of staff in the first instance. Outside of those meetings you should continue to treat them with the exact same level of professional respect as your most talented staff. No one would want to work in a school where the photocopying queue know you haven't marked your books or that you are the subject of a parental complaint, and this certainly isn't the indicative of the ethical culture we're trying to create. As with positive phone calls home, it can be very effective to deliberately praise or thank your colleagues who continue to work hard or even just make you laugh. When you are new to it (and even when you're not!), challenging underperformance can preoccupy you. Taking the time to seek out the positives helps to keep your mindset positive and a kind email or comment can genuinely make your colleagues feel more valued and appreciated. And isn't that what we're here for?

Other inevitable terrain you'll need to traverse in leadership is disagreeing with others, whether they are those you lead or your direct line management. Again, we can channel Jacinda and seek to disagree kindly. So even in the most intense meeting where you vehemently oppose the views of your colleague, as a leader know that this needn't leave the meeting. Dissent is often helpful in clarifying your decisions and eliminating unconscious bias. One litmus test of leadership is how you negotiate challenges to your ideas or beliefs and whether you can disagree on a professional level only. Jacinda can disagree without demonising and so can you. The disagreement may be inevitable but allowing to dwell on the disagreement and let it affect you outside of the meeting is a choice. Again, finding ways to outweigh the negative parts of the job is crucial for your longevity in the profession.

Be positively more Ardern by:

▶ Using the plural pronouns such as "we" and "us" as opposed to "I" in order to reinforce unity.

▶ Showing your human side – openly use and acknowledge any experience you've gained as a mother, auntie, godmother, friend to inform your approach.

▶ Promoting, practising and referring to empathy for staff and students alike.

▶ Communicating sincerely by avoiding platitudes and cliches.

Lesson 3: Be Known by Your Deeds[9]

For a leading political figure, Jacinda somehow manages to transcend the politics that may come with the territory. By leading with integrity, she is known for the impact of her actions, her response to crises and her warmth as a leader. In an arena where individuals can be perceived as caring about their own status or power rather than actually doing the job well, Ardern's deeds serve as a testament to her values. It's inevitable that as a teacher and leader you will encounter some form of professional politics at some stage in your career. In the school setting it is vital that you are not seen to succeed by virtue of politics, luckily, we can draw on Jacinda to keep your professional identity distinct from the political mire.

Sometimes leaders' actions can be misinterpreted as political – often because it may serve the agenda of others. For example, staff within schools can often (knowingly or otherwise) fall into specific camps. As a leader it's important that this is not perceived to influence your practice. For example, the scenario where someone is promoted because "their face fits" may be recognisable to you. It's understandable why someone who hasn't been successful at interview might prefer to choose this narrative over acknowledging that another candidate simply had more to offer, but in truth this is a method used to deflect from the fact that someone else had more of what the school needed. Again, Jacinda's approach offers us the key to diffusing such situations: Integrity and emotional intelligence are key. Integrity which can be deployed to ensure that staff see why and how you've made such decisions, and emotional intelligence to execute this fairly.

And if your actions are perceived as political despite your best efforts, remind yourselves (and anyone else who needs to hear it) that we come to work to serve our students and anything that distracts us from that is little-more than white noise. If staff choose to put their energy into bemoaning who had the last tea-bag as opposed to boosting their students' life chances, then this is what they'll be known for by their colleagues. You, however, can go full-Ardern and ensure that the actions that define you better reflect your dedication to improving student attainment and supporting your colleagues.

In seeking to unite where others divide, empathising where others criticise and to offering vulnerability where others deploy deflection, Ardenism shows us that there is another way of leading; one that reflects our changing appetite for political rhetoric and offers us a masterclass in winning the trust of the masses. Ironically, Jacinda's proven that this is an effective model of leadership which puts the needs of others before her own ego and somehow this results in the very adulation she doesn't want or need, and isn't that the very place to be?

Case Study

Mrs C is a headteacher of a large middle school in the West Midlands whose approach to value-driven mirrors Jacinda's. Early in her career, Mrs C experienced a range of divisive leadership approaches which shaped her as a professional, and later as a leader. For example, one leader pit her against another practitioner which led to unhealthy competition and resentment. Another created a culture of fear in which staff weren't so much buying in, but complying for fear of falling out of favour. Though Mrs C thrived and progressed in spite of these climates, like Jacinda she made a conscious choice to "do leadership differently" as she approached her own tenure as a head.

During some externally ran CPD (continual professional development), Mrs C experienced an epiphany which unknowingly shaped the headteacher she would later become. The epiphany in question was the trainer's claim that staff, and not students are the most important stakeholders in any school setting – a sentiment which was very much at odds with widely held beliefs in the profession, and the personal philosophy held by Mrs C. The course facilitator went on to explain that while students should always at be at the forefront of leaders' practice, one of the best ways to ensure students have the most meaningful school experience is by proxy via staff wellness. The current onus on staff wellbeing was then unheard of, and Mrs C was sold on this approach way before it was an Ofsted focus.

Some years later when beginning her headship, Mrs C found that treating staff with high levels of respect and integrity, while not considered to be evolutionary, was completely revolutionary and fundamental to her mission to bring about a whole-school culture with staff welling at its centre (which is très Ardern). There were several conscious choices that Mrs C made in order to facilitate this: clear lines of accountability were established so that when difficult conversations had to take place staff weren't caught off-guard. Mrs C also made her high expectations explicit as well as detailing what this looks liked in practice, as well as modelling the positive ethos she expected of others.

Additionally, staff were given designated social space and time to connect and communicate, wellbeing champions were appointed to feedback to the leadership team and subsequent staff were ostensibly recruited based on the school's values as opposed to prior experience. Mrs C also handwrites personal notes of thanks to all staff at the end of each academic year and fights to ensure that support staff are held in the same esteem as teachers.

By raising the profile of staff wellbeing and ensuring a humane model of leadership, Mrs C found that staff retention increased, as well as an uptake in staff engagement with CPD, more enrichment opportunities were offered, this later triangulated with student voice which indicated that students were finding their school experience to be more enjoyable. To Mrs C, being value-driven is essentially leading with integrity, demonstrably valuing and championing school staff as much as its students. By using inexpensive school-wide strategies that simply invest in people à la Arden, the eventual return on students was unexpectedly enormous.

Ways to bring the Jacinda to your workplace:

▶ Avoid gossip and conjecture, speak truthfully and openly but only to those it concerns.

▶ Ensure that everything you do is framed by student impact.

▶ Be compassionate to others – including yourself.

▶ Challenge the narrative that women about to take, or returning from, maternity leave is at the expense of them being able to do their jobs.

▶ Refer to big ideas such as values more than you refer to minutiae.

Look for the Jacinda Ardern archetype within your school/ network and note how she:

▶ Is heavily invested in the success of others.

▶ Is able to spot a lack of integrity intuitively, though is unlikely to pass comment on this.

▶ Is not approval-driven and doesn't need affirmation, but receives it regardless.

▶ Is incredibly empathetic and feels everything very deeply.

Final Thought

Being led by integrity and decency may not seem overly revolutionary, but just like Jacinda herself, the impact of this should not be underestimated.

Notes

1 Champman, M. (2020) *Jacinda Ardern: A New Kind of Leader*. Carlton: Schwartz.

2 Ainge Roy, E. (2018) Jacinda Ardern Makes History with Baby Neve at UN General Assembly. *The Guardian*, 24 September. Available at www.theguardian.com/world/2018/sep/25/jacinda-ardern-makes-history-with-baby-neve-at-un-general-assembly (accessed 28 February 2021).

3 Brotheridge, C. (2019) *Brave New Girl: Seven Steps to Confidence*. London: Penguin, p. 176.

4 Blackwell, G. (2020) Jacinda Ardern: Political Leaders Can Be Both Empathetic and Strong. *The Guardian*, 30 May. Available at www.theguardian.com/world/2020/may/31/jacinda-ardern-political-leaders-can-be-both-empathetic-and-strong (accessed 28 February 2021).

5 McKeever, V. (2020) New Zealand Leader Jacinda Ardern Takes 20% Pay Cut Due to Coronavirus. CNBC, 15 April. Available at www.cnbc.com/2020/04/15/coronavirus-new-zealand-leader-jacinda-ardern-takes-20percent-pay-cut.html (accessed 28 February 2021).

6 BBC (2018) Jacinda Ardern Holds Back Tears in Apology to Family of Murdered Tourist Grace Millane. BBC, 10 December. Available at www.bbc.co.uk/news/av/world-asia-46504725 (accessed 12 February 2021).

7 Relman, E. (2018) The New Zealand Prime Minister is the First World Leader to Bring Her Baby to the UN and the Internet Can't Get Enough. *Business Insider*, 25 September. Available at www.businessinsider.com/baby-at-the-un-new-zealand-prime-minister-jacinda-arderns-photos-2018-9?r=US&IR=T (accessed 15 February 2021).

8 Britton, B. (2019) New Zealand PM Full Speech: This Can Only Be Described as a Terrorist Attack. CNN, 15 March. Available at https://edition.cnn.com/2019/03/15/asia/new-zealand-jacinda-ardern-full-statement-intl/index.html (accessed 12 February 2021).

9 Luscombe, B. (2020) A Year After Christchurch, Jacinda Ardern Has the World's Attention. How Will She Use It? *Time*, 20 February. Available at https://time.com/5787443/jacinda-ardern-christchurch-new-zealand-anniversary (accessed 14 February 2021).

QUEEN VI AND ACCOUNTABILITY:

Kim Kardashian

[verb] The act of striving to achieve outrageous goals, extreme ambition especially in relation to task or process.

See also: striving, succeeding.

> " I might be an ECT, but I am going to Kim Kardashian-West a TLR opportunity. "

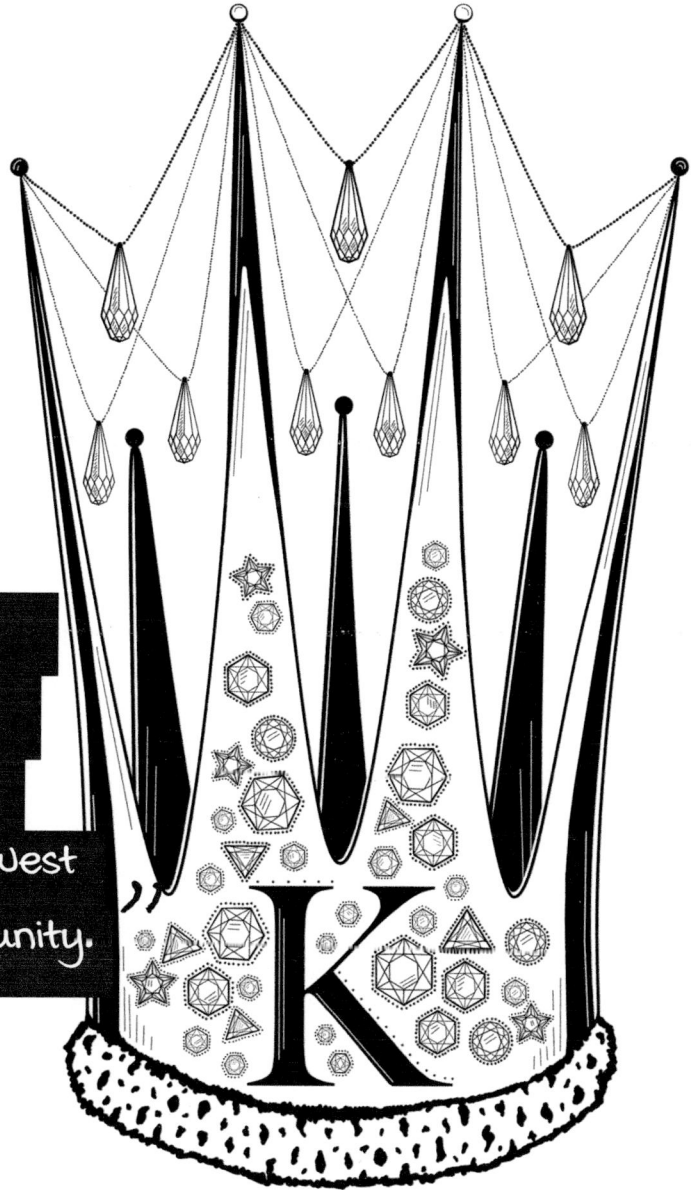

DOI: 10.4324/9781003182474-7

KK's fate as a global icon and socially permissive superstar seems to have been long-fated. Growing up in Calabasas, Los Angeles very much within the proximity of the fame and glamour she would later come to epitomise, Kim was never more than a degree or two of separation from bona fide celebrity. The second daughter of the now famous Kardashian/Jenner dynasty, it now seems abundantly clear that Kim's eventual success isn't only a result of her privilege and pedigree but also her prescience.

As both a result of her time, and a progressive influence upon society, Kim's sheer tenacity, business acumen and apparent unending hunger to succeed is truly laudable. Ultimately Kim has redefined success in such a way that her impact is measurable, (followers, sales, re-tweets) in many ways transcending conventional talent, or at least matching it. It's also clear that Kim is self-aware enough to know that her success is not solely a result of God-given ability, but is actually a result of instinct, hard work and (perhaps above all) ambition. No wonder it's hard to keep up!

Los Angeles lineage aside, it would be remiss to underestimate Kim K's accomplishments or to think of her as a mere product. In truth, one of her USPs is that she has far more agency and autonomy than the average micro-managed celebrity; meaning that she can take far more credit in owning her own success . . . and there is a great deal of credit to share. Forbes estimates Kim's net worth to be over one billion dollars[1] and as the fourth most followed woman on Twitter[2] she has smashed glass ceilings, expectations and sales targets in the process. Not bad for a woman whose first step towards globalisation was organising Paris Hilton's wardrobe.

Recently however, Kim's approach feels less about self-promotion and more about philanthropy. In 2018 she announced that she wished to pursue a career in law – something entirely familiar to her as her late father (in)famously served as part of the defence team for OJ Simpson and had his own successful law career[3] – long before his surname was synonymous with cosmetics and contouring – undoubtedly inspiring Kim's passion for justice. Similarly, Kim has used her platform to champion causes close to her heart, such as the Armenian genocide and gun crime bringing socio-political issues to the attention of her audience and multi-million followers. Most recently, she has been campaigning for criminal justice reform and has successfully fought for clemency for prisoners on death row.[4] By literally saving lives, Kim's success also reminds us that true power and influence is not defined by how it is obtained, but how it is used and that ultimately the only limit on your own success should be your own vision and ambition.

Often thought of negatively in teaching, accountability is vastly underrated. Far from being seen as a performance-management-shaped-stick to beat you, it can actually serve to ensure that you receive the recognition you deserve. Enabling you, like Kim, to own your own success and forge a credible path into leadership and beyond. So here Kim will school us in proving yourself with metric, using evidence to ensure you receive the recognition you deserve, and why your spirt animal needn't be a Kardashian in order to build your own professional brand.

Lesson 1: Learn from Everything You Do[5]

The most obvious takeaway lesson from the success of KK is that being able to quantify your own success is inextricably linked with your leadership credibility. Teaching offers us myriad metric in order to quantify impact, from conventional sources of data such as performance management or student outcomes to more holistic indicators such as Behaviour for Learning data, attendance figures and student voice. Combining hard and soft data to build up a picture of typicality is a common practice within schools, and a technique you can commandeer to gain leverage for negotiation and subsequent opportunities.

As a practitioner, you will have (knowingly or otherwise) begun to create your own professional brand. To develop this further we can commandeer Kim's approach to creating an aesthetic narrative can and apply this to your classroom, consider your classroom layout, displays and resources for example. What do these communicate wordlessly on your behalf? In the same way, EduTwitter or LinkedIn can be used as an extension of your 'brand' in the classroom, think of them as a virtual CV which prospective employers can use as a point of reference in order to gauge the impact you have had in your career thus far. Also, be aware of your USP – the selling point unique and specific to you, for example are you the go-to teacher to support with behaviour, or are you the master of engagement? Perhaps you excel with the most-able or perhaps you are the ultimate differentiation aficionado. Whatever it is, find your niche, own it and then find ways to evidence it.

Before social media, a great deal of credence was given to the media coverage received by celebrities – journalists had the power to make or break a career in their reporting of specific individuals. However, the genesis of social media has given public figures greater ownership of their own narrative – something Kim mastered way back. In the same way, you can control the narrative within your own career and classroom which is an essential part of creating a positive ethos for your pupils. For example, if you have a class who struggle to complete their homework on time it would be easy to bemoan this fact to the students in a hope to impress upon them the importance of getting homework done by the deadline. However, the students may take this on board as part of their collective identity and it can make them feel like not doing homework is the norm for their class which could lead to apathy and a culture of low aspiration.

Equally, you may also choose to control the narrative with a particularly able class to develop the ethos that they are so successful because they work hard, because they consistently behave in line with your expectations, because they demonstrate resilience . . . whichever traits you want to highlight, edit your narrative so that you are always worth reinforcing with the class in question (see also Queen V, Lesson 2). This will ensure that this positive narrative resonates with the students and forms part of their shared identity. If the students are left to determine their own narrative, students in the same class could interpret the fact that they are doing well as not being sufficiently challenged or they need to be moved up a set which can create tension and workload when liaising with the child's parents.

Editing the content and messages that you share with your class can help keep the mood positive in your lessons and keep your classes on side, in the same way that Kim's Instagram feed likely showcases her life and career in its best light. You'd probably choose the most flattering filter for your selfies and your classes deserve the same from the way you speak to, and about them. Telling your class that they're your favourite, making them think that you chose them for your Performance Management observation because they're so advanced, pointing out to your year 8 class that the work they're covering is actually GCSE content or gloating about what a lovely, well-behaved class you have to whomever drops into your lesson are all easy ways to rose-tint your teaching. Narrative in the profession is pervasive, so too is the narrative of your career, therefore in doing this, position yourself as a leader – select which aspects of your practice you wish to accentuate, know your USP and channel Kim to build your brand.

Lesson 2: You Can't React to Everything[6]

Certainly, Kim is also a seasoned pro when it comes to courting controversy. No matter the scandal, Kim is seemingly unphased and seldom seen to lose her cool. Back in the land of teaching, overcoming obstacles is as inevitable as Ofsted, and yet another absolutely essential facet of leadership. In the same way that Kim doesn't allow temporary setbacks to prevent her from achieving her goal and turns obstacles into opportunities, the same resolve is required by educational leaders. Staff absence, changing impact measures, variations in parental engagement – Teaching has its own unique pressures and obstacles. While all effective leaders experience setbacks, they're not defined by them. In times of crisis the role of leaders could be likened to cabin crew during a flight, when experiencing turbulence, we may look to them for reassurance – the likelihood being that if they're calm, we are. Likewise, the roles of school leaders during a crisis should be seen as an opportunity to allay fear and alarm which in turns enables staff to respond with similar poise and precision, something Kim has nailed.

Similarly, as teachers we have hundreds (if not thousands) of moments across a term where we may need to conceal what we're thinking or feeling for the good of the students in front of them. A student makes an inappropriate comment that you find funny but you don't let it show on your face because you don't want to encourage the behaviour; a student makes a safeguarding disclosure to you and you mask the worry from your face to try to make them feel at ease; one of your top performing year 9s tells you that they're not picking your subject for GCSE and you hide your disappointment; a student gives a wrong answer and you make sure that you don't look bemused to avoid knocking their confidence . . . there will be myriad scenarios in which you may need to channel your inner Kardashian and remain composed.

Keeping your cool is also fundamental in behaviour management. No matter how Kardashian-Christmas-card-photoshoot the vibe of the class, you cannot allow this to affect your demeanour, it's our experience that students may find it funny when a teacher has lost their temper, and can delight in watching the teachers' frustration manifest itself in shouting. Equally, this can also be bad PR if a colleague happens to be walking past mid-outburst or if the class next door also hears. While it's obviously important to deal with challenging behaviour, it's rarely the most effective outcome to lose your temper and certainly not how Kim would react.

Something else we can learn from Kim is that she owns the controversy which occasionally comes with the territory: the 72-day marriage, accusations of cultural appropriation, being robbed at gun points. Being composed doesn't mean that you don't learn from the low points and ignore they lessons they teach you, it simply means that those moments do not become part of your highlight reel.

Respond to criticism like a Kardashian:

▶ Acknowledge it professionally, but take care not to assume too much responsibility or apologise needlessly – a phrase like "I'm sorry to hear that, let me have a think about how we can move forwards" can be helpful in achieving this.

▶ Don't be defensive, instead take the time to reflect on whether the criticism is founded before responding.

▶ Be careful not to give negativity too much oxygen, don't let it distract you from your wider goals.

▶ Take negative feedback as a tool to raise your game if necessary – but only if it has merit.

Lesson 3: Put in the Effort to Get What You Want[7]

Strategy and vision are ultimately the things which separate leadership from management, things which Kim had in spades long before she had the credibility and success which followed. While we can't say for sure whether as a comparatively lowly socialite Kim planned for world domination, it's certainly clear that her success is not accidental. Perhaps you're waiting for someone to notice that you harness seemingly outrageous Kardashian-esque ambitions . . . ultimately you needn't wait for opportunities to arise to indicate your intentions. So, set out your stall with your mentor, line manager, SLT link or appraiser. Communicate your aims to progress and ask for opportunities to lead, even (and especially) if unpaid. Then when you're inevitably given a project to lead howsoever modest, make sure you can evidence impact. That may be something as conventional as student outcomes, but it may also be online views of a school marketing video, sixth form applications or even attendance at parents' evening. Where possible work from the evidential outcome backwards so that you are intentionally building up an unarguable body of evidence to illustrate your impact.

Being proactive within the profession can be challenging, the relentless pace of the profession can sometimes necessitate a more reactive approach. Howsoever busy your role, try to be seen to go the extra mile as much as possible. Rather than waiting for someone to notice your talent and dedication be your own advocate à la Kim: Ask to shadow staff who have the role you'd like, identify appropriate CPD, ask to observe leadership interviews. Wear your ambition proudly and ensure your actions match your intentions. The fashion world and media may have openly mocked Kim in the beginning of her career and she has since landed multiple Vogue covers[8]. Have your eyes on the end goal, howsoever initially ambitious and seemingly unattainable. With that said, you can't skip straight to the proactive part, successful leadership in education must always begin with successfully leading your own classroom. Undoubtedly, the first indication of your ability to lead will be apparent in how you manage your classes. So, in stepping up to leadership, first make sure that your own classes/ marking/ data entry are in order as this is still your biggest headline in terms of your own PR.

While it's unlikely that Kim is would ever apply for a TLR role, if she did, what would her covering letter look like? What first impression would she create? If her social media output is anything to go by, her application would be precisely rooted in evidence and full of proof of her impact. In the same way that her Instagram page is intentionally curated, you can construct your own career highlight reel. Furthermore, Kim's online presence is consciously constructed and wordlessly communicates her values and brand. The same approach can be applied to writing a covering letter or job application; select the relevant or most impressive aspects of your accomplishments to ensure that you put forward the very best version of you, positioning you as a leader and where possible substantiating this with quantitative evidence.

As a mother of four, model, entrepreneur and aspiring lawyer, Kim is succeeding both unapologetically and intentionally on her own terms. Her journey from socialite to global brand is nothing short of remarkable, and howsoever unexpected or apparently unconventional in nature the journey, it's hard not to marvel at the destination.

Widely thought to be the mother of social media, as a simultaneous product, brand and advert, Kim not only broke the internet; she basically owns it.

Case Study

Miss B is the head of a large English department and her experiences of accountability early in her career unquestionably shaped her as a leader. Back when Kim was still working in retail, Miss B was in her second year of teaching. Miss B was surprised (and inwardly horrified) when she was allocated a very difficult, low-ability class within her inner-city secondary school. Notably what followed occurred back in the days of where the accountability framework prioritised C grades in English Language over overall attainment. In this particular school students sat their GCSE in English Language in year 10 and only the top sets would go onto study Literature in year 11 – thankfully educational reform has made this practice impossible, but this was not an uncommon strategy adopted by schools at the time.

Miss B's class were a typical bottom set, with high levels of SEND, Pupil Premium and EAL and were identified as potential NEETS (students not in education, employment or training). Though the students were taught GCSE media studies, the unofficial mandate was that students should just be "occupied" until study leave – as had always happened unchallenged in previous years and for the parallel set (incidentally deemed so challenging that only the Head of Department would teach them). This did not sit well with Miss B, who felt strongly that the students would benefit from the opportunity to be entered for the qualification in earnest and, and was in possession of some promising data which suggested that the students stood a good chance of succeeding in the qualification. The Head of Department subsequently dismissed her request for the simple fact that some relatively low-grade GCSE grades in a foundation subject would have a negligible impact on the school's headline figures.

Not to be deterred, and showing some indication of the tenacious leader she would later become, Miss B seized a positive learning walk with the class in question as an opportunity to showcase their abilities. The learning walk just happened to be with the headteacher who was struck by the class's motivation, their commitment and their attitudes to learning. When Miss B was able to produce a detailed mark book and sample coursework pieces to triangulate with the success of the learning walk, (and recognising the powerful impact that GCSE success would have on the students' lives), the head insisted that the class were entered for the qualification, and every single student received a grade of some description, for many of the class it was their highest grade. Some years later a student from the erstwhile media class contacted Miss B to say that her poor behaviour at school had stemmed from her difficulties with reading, but bolstered by her grade in media studies, she had re-sat GCSE English at college and had become the first in her family to receive a GCSE in English, serving to prove that the power of believing in someone should never be underestimated.

As for Miss B, she never forgot the power that came with being able to support her innate instincts with quantitative data, something which informs her practice to date. She is now an advocate for using data to facilitate difficult conversations, to hold staff to account and to strive for better outcomes for students (howsoever holistic) – demonstrating how this can de-personalise and disarm even the most senior members of staff. Like Kim, Miss B showed that while being seen to succeed is great, being able to evidence your success is irrefutable.

Ways to channel your inner KK and win at work:

▶ Wear your success like Kim wears Balmain – openly, unapologetically and everywhere.

▶ Allow yourself to be underestimated if it means that you are given the autonomy to develop.

▶ Under promise and over deliver, always seek to exceed expectations.

▶ Be meticulous and detail-driven in everything you lead.

▶ Network with the intention of elevating others as you ascend.

Look for the KK archetype within your school/ network and note how she:

▶ Has wildly ambitious career goals and will likely fulfil them.

▶ Has a strong work ethic reinforced by clear boundaries.

▶ Executes tasks with precision and can evidence her impact.

▶ Displays innate instincts which may transcend academia.

Final Thought

Like her shapewear and silhouette, everything about KK is measured and controlled, curating your career in this way will give it real backbone.

Notes

1   Friedman, M., Gonzales, E. & Sanchez, C. (2021) Here's How Much Every Member of the Kardashian Family is Worth. *Harper's Bazaar*, 6 April. Available at www.harpersbazaar.com/celebrity/latest/a22117965/kardashian-family-net-worth (accessed 28 August 2021).

2   Boyd, J. (2021) The Most Followed Accounts on Twitter. *Brandwatch*, 24 August. Available at www.brandwatch.com/blog/most-twitter-followers (accessed 28 August 2021).

3   Porterfield, C. (2020) Kim Kardashian Says OJ Simpson Murder Trial "Tore My Family Apart" in Rare Admission. *Forbes*, 21 October. Available at www.forbes.com/sites/carlieporterfield/2020/10/21/kim-kardashian-west-says-oj-simpson-murder-trial-tore-my-family-apart-in-rare-admission/?sh=4265eb572d61 (accessed 28 August 2021).

4   Rees, A. (2020) "I Wish I Had Paid Attention Sooner": Kim Kardashian West on Her Justice Project and Quest for Apolitical Prison Reform. *Time*, 3 April. Available at https://time.com/5815300/kim-kardashian-justice-project-prison-reform (accessed 28 August 2021).

5   Ahlgrim, C. (2018) 21 Essential Quotes from Kim Kardashian. *Insider*, 19 October. Available at www.insider.com/kim-kardashian-best-quotes-2018-10 (accessed 28 August 2021).

6   Ibid.

7   Ibid.

8   Van Meter, J. (2019) The Awakening of Kim Kardashian. *Vogue*, 10 April. Available at www.vogue.com/article/kim-kardashian-west-cover-may-2019 (accessed 28 August 2021).

QUEEN VII
AND
LEADERSHIP:

Malala Yousafzai

*[Noun] The mentor who leads
by elevating others, a prolific
leader who pioneers
on behalf of others.*

See also: guru, nurturer.

"
I think my ECT
mentor will proofread
my covering letter,
she is a real malala.

DOI: 10.4324/9781003182474-8

You know you're talking about an actual legend when you can refer to them mononymously and it's clear who you're talking about. So in the same way that we have a Beyoncé and an Adele, we have Malala. In fact, her very name is loaded with cultural subtext which perhaps foreshadowed the incredible life she would later lead. That name was inspired by Malalai of Maiwand (1861–1880)[1] – a historically significant Pashto folklore heroine who is said to have inspired Afghan soldiers into victory, before being shot dead by a British soldier during the second Anglo-Afghan war. The parallels between our Malala and her namesake are clear, as is the fact that it was quite obviously her destiny to change the world – especially for females.

As a Pakistani activist and advocate, Malala Yousafzai is a symbol of hope amid tyranny and oppression. Where most 17-year-olds are sitting their theory test and perhaps trying to master the Harvard referencing system, Malala was making history by becoming the youngest ever Nobel Prize laureate,[2] and the second only Pakistan-born recipient scoring her all the queen points in the process!

Born in July 1997, Malala is the eldest of three siblings, and only daughter, of Ziauddin Yousafzai and Tor Pekai Yousafzai. Malala's father was a teacher and ran a school for girls, but in 2008 the Taliban seized control of her hometown in Swat Valley and subsequently banned girls' education – one of many in a litany of restrictions on citizens' freedom. During this time Malala spoke out publicly against the prohibition of girls' education, encouraged by her father, who was already an established activist.[3]

It's widely documented that Malala was shot by the Taliban in a targeted-attack on her way home from school in 2012 when she was aged just 15. However, far from murdering her, the extremists unwittingly gave Malala a platform from which she was able to exact change on a far bigger scale. In fact, as a direct consequence of her shooting, 2 million people signed the Right to Education Bill, which led to it becoming ratified.[4] An own goal for terrorism and a seismic step in terms of Malala's ascent into the land of queenery. Mic drop.

For many, this would be the end of the story, or certainly the end of their activism but not for Malala. Besides publicly forgiving her attackers (which in itself was huge), Malala took the additional publicity gained by her shooting and deflected the limelight onto her selfless campaign to facilitate equal education for girls. She founded the Malala Fund, which birthed the Education Champion Network so that Malala's impact wasn't simply confined to her country of birth, but to anywhere where education for females was not already a given.[5] It's hard to comprehend how so much good can come from an act of terror, but Malala reminds us of the importance of thinking big and acting with intent. Who finer to learn from, than the girl who turned a shooting into an uprising?

Malala's personal success post-shooting has also been astounding, in 2014 she moved to the UK to reunite with her family and continue her studies – the very thing she had striven for from the onset. In 2020 Malala's narrative arc peaked when she graduated with a degree in Philosophy, Politics and Economics. The living embodiment of her passion for education fulfilled, oh and did we mention this was actual Oxford University?[6] An astounding accomplishment on its own, but even more so in the context of the preceding obstacles.

Fearless yet composed, Malala does not present as a stereotypical leader, she is humble and unassuming, she has no tricks up her sleeve to dazzle us, she doesn't use smoke and mirrors to deflect and she is not democratically elected . . . and yet her success serves as a reminder that the value of a leader is ultimately determined by the impact they have on others, and what they stand for as opposed to their political rhetoric. Though Malala can legitimately state that she picked a fight with the Taliban and won, it's the way in which this was also a wider victory for freedom and justice that really defines her leadership.

I Am a Leader

Arguably leadership is the product of our other principles put together, but we want to explore a specific aspect of leadership here, and that is the responsibility we have to channel Malala and when we get any form of platform within school or otherwise, by getting behind other women in the profession, supporting them and empowering them to lead, the importance of this cannot be overstated. There are real barriers out there to the progression of women, and we are all charged with addressing this injustice. If Malala shows us anything it's that the smallest action can have the biggest of consequences, so here's how you can contribute to the ripple effect and empower other women.

It's not entirely selfless to get behind others, since success of those you lead, is success for you too, in the same way that Malala can claim credit for the millions of girls who have been educated as a direct result of her activism. Malala is not leader-centric in her approach, instead she uses her own achievements as a means of allowing others to shine. This is the curious thing with leadership, it can both come from, and not be about you at the same time. So in the same way that your entire class exceeding expectations in terms of data reflects your success and yet is also personal success for the pupils who've earned it, the success of your team clearly reflects you.

Lesson 1: The Importance of Our Voices[7]

As teachers, what we say is important. We impart knowledge throughout the school day (and sometimes, inadvertently, beyond that too); if we're lucky, what we say is remembered. Teachers have a natural platform on which to share their voices, which can be a double-edged sword. When you ask a question to a class and a student responds by quoting you verbatim from a lesson last week, it's a fantastic feeling and a nice reminder that your voice is one of the most effective tools at a teacher's disposal for transferring knowledge. It would be a dreadful feeling, however, if you were to snap at a student, say the wrong thing and have the student quote you verbatim at your parents' evening appointment. The same is true for your colleagues; months after a conversation with a colleague you can find that something you said really stuck with them – hopefully for a good reason!

As a leader in a school, the importance of your words is amplified. Comments you've made may be discussed between colleagues, being paraphrased and distorted as they spread. This makes it even more important to choose your words carefully. Leaders are inevitably going to have to say things that others don't like at some point and when this happens it's important that your words convey precisely what you mean. Being a burgeoning queen, you'll no doubt be communicating with the interests of the students in mind so it will be important for that to come across. When you're explaining an idea or concept to a class, you'll no doubt have thought through your explanation, perhaps accompanied it with an analogy to make sure it's as lucid as possible. The same is true when communicating with your colleagues; if you're using your voice to convey some-thing important (and you probably are!) then winging your explanation opens you up to having your voice misinterpreted or to waffling and watering down what you're actually trying to say.

Unleashing your most Malala-esque tendencies involves choosing what to use your voice for. All staff in schools are influential, whether they intend to be or not. Your voice can be used to celebrate the successes of students and staff, to diffuse stressful or diffi-cult situations, to raise issues constructively with the relevant people . . . but it can also be used to idly gossip about things you know nothing about or to moan to whoever will listen. As a queen, you'd hopefully choose the former, understanding the power of your voice and how it will likely affect those around you.

There are times where using your voice can be challenging, where it would be eas-ier to say nothing or to simply say what someone else wants to hear. Often thoughts will go through your head while in a meeting, for instance, which don't get heard. Some-times this might be the right call but sometimes those ideas and thoughts are definitely worth voicing. Malala's voice is used to promote education, to correct inequalities and injustices and if in that moment your thoughts are serving the same purposes then they're certainly worth sharing.

Lesson 2: Stand with Your Sisters[8]

John Donne postulated that "no man is an island".[9] While this is undoubtedly true, we can't help but wonder what the equivalent geographical analogy is for women. Are we continents? Peninsulas? Tectonic plates? Certainly, as female practitioners and leaders, our power and strength is amplified when we unite. Malala shows us how powerful we can be commutatively and exactly what is possible when women come together.

Collaboration is integral; the sharing of ideas as well as working with others – especially working with and learning from, those whose area of expertise and talents differ from your own in vital for your own leadership and in order to move your school forwards. But this is more than collaboration – this is solidarity with your fellow female practitioners, regardless of where they are in their career, which is essential to cultivate.

The support that staff receive as novices can have a huge effect on their career overall. As teachers we are absolutely ace at nurturing talent in the classroom and we have the same opportunity (and obligation) to utilise this skillset to develop staff too. What form might this take? Mentoring is an obvious means of channelling Malala, whether formally or otherwise, your school may use a coaching model which enables staff to learn from other practitioners without a hierarchical superior in the equation, or perhaps by virtue of the ECF (early career framework). Whatever the platform in your school, perhaps a game-changing approach could be to simply assume that all women entering the profession have the eventual aim to lead, because certainly this is the unconscious bias we have towards men.

Now, of course there is the danger that this member of staff will be so flipping skilled and employable that they take all you have taught them elsewhere and it won't benefit your school at all. The better you are at nurturing staff, the higher the risk this presents. Though if staff feel valued and supported (which will undoubtedly be the case if they are correctly mentored) surely they are more likely to stay? And when some of the staff in whom you have invested receive external promotion – because this will happen – wish them well in the knowledge that they are likely to empower those they lead. So whether the talent you've managed goes or stays, you will have contributed to more women in leadership roles in teaching and the ripple effect and is thus a win for us all.

Standing with your sisters is more than just supporting the women in school who may be less experienced than you. Those queens with equal and more experience than you are just as in need of support. There is a pervasive myth that women are hardwired to compete and therefore that we are in competition with each other. Like a real-life tabloid "who wore it better?" it's easy to see that women don't benefit from this doctrine, and nor do our respective professions. It would be great to think that women weren't in leadership roles because they had been pipped to the post by supremely talented *other* women, but the data tells us the people in those roles are male. Other women are not career obstacles, this patriarchal narrative poses a bigger threat to your career than Hannah from the History department and her Masters degree and sensational work wardrobe. Viewing your female colleagues with a more compassionate, supportive lens helps everyone.

Lesson 3: One Teacher at a Time[10]

Our lesson here is inspired by the speech in which Malala said "One child, one teacher, one book and one pen can change the world" – a sentiment which surely resonates with all of us. Malala's position here is clearly a nod to the power of education as the sum of wider socio-political forces and also indicative of the marginal gains we see every day at the chalk face.

Adopting this piecemeal approach is helpful, because often in teaching it takes some time for the bigger picture to emerge. For example, the child who struggles to stay in their chair is likely to begin by successfully completing their starter activity in situ before winning a headteacher's award, though the former has undoubtedly resulted in the latter. As a profession, we are trained to chase the marginal gains as we know that this is always a precursor to success on a larger scale, often success which transcends a school and the impact can be seen on a community, a city and sometimes even further still.

Back in the land of leadership, the same can be said of the small-scale victories we can rack up to empower women into positions of responsibility. If we each made it our business to seek out and champion one great female teacher per academic year, this would eventually amount to radical change. And if every one of your protégées did the same and so on, this could quite conceivably be enough to change the world à la Malala. Obviously, we are not suggesting that you champion a teacher for simply being a woman, but that you champion teachers who should be leaders and their gender (or issues stemming indirectly from this) may be the only reason they are not.

The extent to which women are underrepresented in educational leadership is endemic and undoubtedly big changes are needed at decision-making level if the issues around recruitment and retention of female talent are to be resolved. However, in the same way that one 15-year-old girl making a stand was an unlikely way to change the face of education, as teachers we can never know the extent of our reach nor the full extent of the impact we have on others, and perhaps this is doubly true of leaders of teachers.

Although commandeered by many as a symbol of courage, freedom and possibility, Malala is a great example of the ripple effect in action. Even before she had a platform, she was selflessly devoted to elevating others. Similarly, she is also a reminder of the power of education as a systemic means of elevating others, something easily taken for granted within the western world. As teachers and leaders we can be more Malala and use our own influence for the benefit of others.

Case Study

Mrs D has recently retired from her role as executive headteacher and CEO of a primary Multi-Academy Trust who has channelled Malala in her championing of women throughout her career. Prior to becoming a teacher Mrs D worked in a senior role in industry, when returning from her second maternity leave, she requested to work part time. While she was permitted to work fewer days, this was on the condition that she relinquished her additional responsibility – to which she reluctantly agreed. Some years later when Mrs D worked full time again, she was frustrated to learn that career-wise her previous leadership experience wasn't recognised and if she wanted to progress into a leadership post again, in effect her career would have to start again from the bottom up in spite of her previously held role.

This apparent injustice stayed with Mrs D so when she joined the teaching profession and found herself as a headteacher a mere decade later, she made it her business to create a culture in which women needn't choose between working flexibly and leading. Mrs D sees teaching as a vocation and believes that women are absolutely integral to the profession. Mrs D also feels strongly that leaders should show flexibility in order to retain strong female staff especially after maternity leave where they are statistically more likely to leave leadership and/or the profession.[11]

One such beneficiary of Mrs D's female-centred approach is an outstanding practitioner who held a TLR as a key stage lead who was returning from maternity leave. Part of the wider expectations of TLR holders within Mrs D's MAT was that they were often required to attend SLT meetings and complete additional duties, something Mrs D's protégées had expressed concerns about prior to having her daughter.

Therefore, Mrs D was not altogether surprised when this practitioner relinquished her TLR and requested to work flexibly so that she could drop and collect her daughter from nursery once a week and to avoid late night SLT meetings with no defined end time. Not only did Mrs D accept the request she also set up a sequence of measures to enable this practitioner to lead without some of the additional expectations which rendered leadership unattractive to a new parent.

Firstly, Mrs D placed the member of staff onto the upper pay scale, and set running the foundation stage as her UP target (in effect, the same pay increase as the TLR). She also set up a morning of dedicated leadership time so that the member of staff could have some semblance of a work life balance in addition to the flexibility she had requested. Beyond this, all staff who are parents in Mrs D's MAT were also offered cover to attend their children's nativities/ assemblies/ sports days, something which was doubtlessly a factor in retaining her outstanding key stage leader.

Other measures Mrs D has put into place in order to invest in strong female staff included mentoring, external CPD and support when applying for promotion even if external and while Mrs D hasn't been able to promote every great female teacher she's led, they have all benefitted from Mrs D's person-centred leadership approach, and often gone on to reciprocate this in other schools, thus amplifying her legacy in the process.

By talent spotting and appointing staff on merit and when-needed exercising flexibility Mrs D was able to create a culture in which women were empowered to lead and subsequently given the resources to succeed, from which students, staff and their families have profited in every sense, Mrs D's approach reminds us that like Malala, great leaders don't create followers, they create more leaders.

Get more Malala for your money by:

▶ Modelling the benefits of leadership to others.

▶ Singing the praises of other women – to them and about them.

▶ Reminding others of the privilege and power of education.

▶ Fighting to ensure that other women are heard and represented.

Look out for the Malala archetype in your school/network and note how:

▶ Her mentoring will go far beyond statutory expectations, and mentees really blossom under her tutorage.

▶ She takes others with her as she rises.

▶ She is more interested in making others look good as opposed to the perception of herself.

▶ Often others are trying to impress her because she has the tools and connections to create opportunity for others.

Final Thought

Pay your professional success forwards with a Malala approach which champions and empowers other women into leadership and beyond.

Notes

1   Dalrymple, W. (2013) Before Malala. *New York Times*, 25 October. Available at www.nytimes.com/2013/10/26/opinion/international/malalas-brave-namesake. html (accessed 4 March 2021).

2 Yousafzai, M. (2014) Nobel Peace Prize Acceptance Speech. Available at https://malala.org/newsroom/archive/malala-nobel-speech (accessed 9 March 2021).

3 Yousafzai, M. (2013) *I Am Malala: The Girl Who Stood up for Education and Was Shot by the Taliban*. New York: Little, Brown, & Company.

4 Fast Company (2017) Five Leadership Lessons from Malala Yousafzai. Available at www.fastcompany.com/3052132/five-leadership-lessons-from-malala-yousafzai (accessed 19 March 2021).

5 Malala.org (2017) The Malala Fund. Available at www.malala.org/malalas-story (accessed 19 March 2017).

6 Emmrich, E. (2020) Nobel Peace Prize Winner Malala Yousafzai Graduates from Oxford. *Vogue*, June 20. Available at www.vogue.com/article/malala-yousafzai-nobel-peace-prize-winner-graduates-from-oxford#:~:text=Nobel%20Peace%20Prize%E2%80%93Winner%20Malala%20Yousafzai%20Graduates%20From%20Oxford&text=Malala%20Yousafzai%2C%20the%20Pakistani%20activist,from%20Oxford%20University%20this%20weekend (accessed 20 March 2021).

7 Yousafzai, M. (2013) *I Am Malala: The Girl Who Stood up for Education and Was Shot by the Taliban*. New York: Little, Brown, & Company.

8 Yousafzai, M. (2013) Sixteenth Birthday Speech at the United Nations. Available at https://malala.org/newsroom/archive/malala-un-speech (accessed 9 March 2021).

9 Donne, J. (1624) No Man Is an Island. Available at https://allpoetry.com/No-man-is-an-island (accessed 18 December 2021).

10 Yousafzai, M. (2013) Speech to UN Assembly. Speakola, 12 July. Available at https://speakola.com/ideas/malala-yousafzai-un-youth-assembly-2013 (accessed 20 March 2021).

11 Department for Education (2018) Factors Affecting Teacher Retention: Qualitative Investigation. Available at https://assets.publishing.service.gov.uk/government/uploads/system/uploads/attachment_data/file/686947/Factors_affecting_teacher_retention_-_qualitative_investigation.pdf (accessed 25 May 2021).

HAPPILY

EVER

AFTER

Here is where we distil the lessons from our queens into a succinct plan of action and ask you to throw out your pebbles and contribute to the ripple effect.

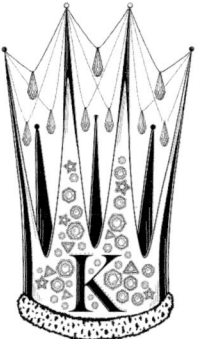

DOI: 10.4324/9781003182474-9

The End?

And so our queens live happily ever after with the power and influence and elevate others, in addition to the ability to continue to excel in their respective fields – not just as archetypes but as fully actualised icons. It may be too soon to gauge the extent of the legacy that these phenomenal women will eventually leave behind, but it's easy to begin to see how they're likely to be remembered by history.

It is our sincere hope that this is not an ending, but a beginning: the point after which leadership and teaching can be seen not as separate roles, but as inextricable parts of the same vocation and therefore a teacher stepping into leadership is not considered to be a "new" role, but rather as a natural continuation of what we do in the classroom.

Our queens have shown us that greatness can sometimes transcend that which is personal. There is nothing to be gained by playing small;[1] similarly, there is very little to be gained by affecting adequacy if you're actually extraordinary – and by the same token by achieving adequate goals if you're capable of something more remarkable. The message from this book is simple: step up and rise up – and when you're up there remember to elevate other women – it's really that straightforward.

In a parallel universe Kim still works in retail, RuPaul works the bars in New York and Michelle took the advice of her career adviser – did not set her sights high and now does the admin for an accountant. Our queens show us that it's not only talent and ability which separate those who lead from those who don't – it begins with a choice to firstly aspire to this. Women need to get to a place where leadership is seen not just as an option, but also an entitlement – and then to develop the confidence to claim and commandeer this without fear. What is there to fear? Not being good enough? Of failing? Of disapproval? We need to let go of the limiting assumptions which have somehow taken root and obliterate them in order to allow possibility and optimism bloom in its place.

Solutions

It's been a conscious choice not to focus on the myriad obstacles to women progressing as leaders in teaching, but rather to explore how such challenges can be overcome – but make no mistake these obstacles present a very real threat to women advancing in the profession. In writing we were struck by recurring themes of fearing disapproval, the desire for flexible working and the chronic (unfounded) lack of collective confidence women seem to have in their own ability – both in and out of teaching. It's time for us to out this, label it as the fallacy it is and work together to bring about real change.

What if you're not good enough? What if you excel? What if you get out of your depth? But also, what if you don't? What if you can't cope? What if you flourish? Choose action over procrastination and possibility over probability. We also need to normalise asking for help and seeking proactive support if it's needed to encourage other women to put themselves forward. Perhaps the biggest pervasive myth is that leaders themselves don't get direction or support; when in fact all leaders are led themselves – especially at senior level, in fact for a leader to "fail", it means that a more senior leader has also failed – which is in absolutely no one's interests.

Though ultimately, it's not enough to simply celebrate women, we need to galvanise this appreciation into action. While organisations such as WomenEd have been making incredible headway in ensuring that women are represented and above all heard at decision making level, among this the power of the individual is key. We'd like to indict all women in the profession to contribute to this movement, wherever and however you can.

And when you are in a position of leadership make it your mission to market this to others, wear leadership lightly, show other women that it is rewarding, enjoyable and fun – because it absolutely is. So that when others are considering leadership, they will see how it can be done enjoyed rather than endured. More than this, make a point of illustrating this to others through interaction, celebration and the narrative you present.

Imagine a future in which schools and education are ran by more queens. How would this be different and similar to the current landscape? What impact would this have on students? On curriculum? On recruitment? On attainment? What eventual rewards could this reap? Imagine an infrastructure in education where the number of female leaders is proportionate to the number of women in the profession. This vision is ours for the taking, and it starts here

Throw Your Pebble

In the words of Queen Elizabeth II's[2] affirmation, it is often the small steps, not the giant leaps that bring about the most lasting change. And isn't that what we signed up for? To this end, your pebble is powerful. Howsoever small or far you throw it. If enough pebbles are thrown the cumulative effect might just be a tidal wave. Throw out your pebble to amplify your impact, throw out your pebble to bring about change, throw out your pebble to empower others – but most of all just throw it and watch the impact grow.

Go queens – you've got this!

Notes

1   Williamson, M. (1996) *A Return to Love*. New York: HarperCollins.
2   Elizabeth II. (2019) Christmas Day Message. Available at www.youtube.com/watch?v=KgvZnxNAThM (accessed 19 August 2021).

Afterword

We wanted to give the final word to our case study queens who have generously given their time and shared a little of their brilliance. These are their top takeaway tips to help you as you step into, or continue to navigate, leadership terrain.

Mrs C

▶ Always be true to yourself. Taking advice from others is great, but you have to figure out your own way as it has to run through your veins if you are going to be able to live and breathe it.

▶ Failure and making mistakes are an inevitable part of growth. Accept, reflect and move forward.

▶ Strong leadership has to be founded on professional trust, as honesty and integrity matter more to others than anything else. If staff see you do what you say you will, trust will form a foundation on which you can build and move forwards.

Mrs F

▶ Always strive to be the most inspiring and effective leader you wish to be but remember to ensure balance as much as possible.

▶ Aim high but remember, "Rome wasn't built in a day".

▶ Leading by example will empower others to grow.

▶ Everyone in a school is a leader; whether this is in their classroom, subject, year group, at lunchtimes, during interventions or leading a whole school. Everyone has valuable contributions to make a school the best it can be; listen to others' ideas, celebrate their ideas and together a vision will be created and embraced.

Mrs D

Aim to Be a Credible Leader

In a primary setting, get to know and understand children's learning and development in the different key stages, take the opportunity to teach in Foundation Stage, Key Stage 1 and upper Key Stage 2. If I had stayed just as a Key Stage 2 teacher and not taken the opportunity to teach in Foundation Stage (though it was a shock going from Year 5 to Reception), I would never have understood the demands and needs of what is required in the Foundation Stage as a Headteacher. This is in terms of staffing, physical resources as well as understanding the pedagogy of phonics, early reading and writing. Also, being a SENCO developed my understanding of autism and dyslexia which as a senior leader was invaluable.

Vision and Values

When you're a headteacher you will obviously have a vision of what you want for your school. Alongside, have a clear set of values – about five – and keep the language simple. The values should be able to link to every possible behaviour and these are a standard for all stakeholders: pupils, staff, parents and governors with the language used consistently by all.

Our big five values:

▶   Take personal responsibility.

▶   Have bouncebackability (resilience).[1]

▶   Set yourself huge goals.

▶   Choose to be positive.

▶   Understand your impact.[2]

Never Stop Reading

Stay abreast with current educational thinking and policy. Read great leadership and pedagogy books. I loved reading the TES weekly, lots of top tips and thinking about education. Build your knowledge of leadership and management, together with pedagogy so that you can be that credible leader.

   Don't forget to read great children's books too, so that you can share excellent literature with the children and staff too.

Training and Excellence in Schools

Go and see great national trainers. For example, if you want knowledge about assessment sign up for Shirley Clarke training; writing – Pie Corbett; behaviour – Paul Dix. Go and see the best, they inspire you. Also, arrange visits to other schools, you can learn something on every visit and in every setting. Never pre-judge, as I've seen inadequate teaching in outstanding schools and outstanding teaching in Special Measures schools.

Mrs P

▶ Assertiveness doesn't make you difficult, and kindness doesn't make you a pushover. They are not mutually exclusive. Great leaders should possess both.

▶ Make peace with the fact that you'll never get everything ticked off your to-do list. Prioritise wisely and treat everybody's time as precious, including your own.

▶ Only apologise if the situation absolutely warrants it. Try thanking people instead. For example, instead of "I'm sorry, but this wasn't what I had in mind", try saying "Thank you for your work on this. I'd like to try X next".

Mrs W

▶ Never make assumptions – refer to the ladder of inference,[3] get the facts, ask the questions.

▶ Be present and listen – no matter how busy you are always make time for a colleague who comes to you with a problem. They chose to speak to you so choose to listen to them.

▶ Take people with you and grow talent, you cannot lead alone.

▶ Beware of toxic influences, don't get drawn into negativity and hold on to your educational beliefs and values.

▶ Leadership is not a race – being an effective leader won't happen overnight, nurture it, be reflective, embrace change, be open to feedback, learn from mistakes, and continue to improve, there is no end point.

▶ Remember you are human, take care of your physical and mental health.

My five-step reflective mantra on facilitating change:

1   Have I reflected on my decision(s)?
2   Is this change meaningful and useful?

3   What are the implications?
4   Have I involved everyone I need in deciding and implementing this change?
5   What will the positive impact of this change be?

Mrs K

▶ Be observant and pay close attention – you don't need to verbally acknowledge everything you see – but make mental notes and allow this to inform evaluation and give you the information that data won't.

▶ Look out for the lower profile and hardworking staff, praise them and develop them as they may not ask for this, nor expect it.

▶ Only speak when it's necessary – this will increase the value of your voice when you do choose to use it.

Miss B

▶ As a leader you may experience cynicism, positivity is a great remedy for this, even better if you are not the source of it!

▶ It's far easier to hold others to account when you model the conduct and commitment you expect of others.

▶ There are worse things in life than experiencing disapproval, the male leaders I work with do not go home and beat themselves up, leadership is much less personal than we tend to assume.

▶ Be relentless in raising standards for students, be as tenacious and ambitious on their behalf as if they were your own.

▶ Always put the students' needs before your own ego!

Notes

1   Cope, A. (2006) *Being Brilliant: The Art of Being Yourself . . . Brilliantly*. Kent: Balloon View.
2   Ibid.
3   Argyris, C. (1990) *Overcoming Organisational Defences: Facilitating Organisational Learning*. Hoboken, NJ: Pearson Education.

Index

accountability 12, 16, 21, 31, 34, 46, 50 52, 55, 60, 86

ambition 23, 60, 64, 86

Ardern, J 4, 50, 51–56, 62

authenticity 11, 17, 11, 34, 46

Behaviour for Learning 25, 34, 52, 53, 61, 62, 65, 84, 85

British monarchy 30, 33

Continuous Professional Development 13, 43, 55, 56, 64

COVID-19 3, 51

curriculum 14, 20, 81

Drag 20, 22, 40

Drag Race 20, 21, 23

Early Career Framework 22, 73

Early Career Teacher 22, 73

EHCP 25, 55

Ethics 3, 16, 21, 22

Feedback 21, 22, 23, 32

Flexible working 16, 35–36 75, 76

GCSE 62, 63, 65, 66

gender 41, 74

governors 15, 20, 36, 84

Harvard University 10, 14

injustice 4, 10, 11, 15, 16, 40, 41, 45, 71, 72, 75

Kardashian, K 4, 6, 60–66, 80

kindness 41, 42, 50

Lady Gaga 4, 5, 6, 40–46

LGBTQ 20, 40

line manager 25, 33, 64

Markle, M 4, 6, 30–36

maternity leave 35, 56, 75

media 10, 11 30, 31, 34, 40, 61, 64

mental health 35, 41, 43, 44, 85

mentoring 20, 73, 75, 76

minorities 6, 14, 41

Multi-Academy Trust 15, 75

NEETs 45, 65

New York 40, 80

Nolan Principles 2, 3, 4, 5

Obama, B 10, 11, 12, 13, 14

Obama, M 4, 6, 10–16, 51, 80

Ofsted 6, 15, 16, 24, 55, 62

Parents 20, 21, 22, 23, 51, 53, 62, 64, 72, 75, 84

patriarchy 5, 50, 73

people pleasing 32, 46

Performance Management 42, 60, 61, 62

politics 10, 11, 14, 50, 51, 54, 55,
71
Princeton University 10, 14
promotion 31, 60, 73, 75
public relations 40, 61, 63
Pupil Premium 15, 22, 23, 40, 44, 45, 52,
64

Queen, HM 81

race 10, 20, 70
Resilience 31, 33, 36, 62, 63, 84
ripple effect 21, 23, 71, 73, 74, 81
Rupaul 4, 6, 20–26, 80

SENCO 15, 16, 24, 25, 84
SEND 15, 16, 41, 52, 65
Senior Leadership Team 25, 33, 64, 75, 81,
84

shared culture 16, 44
social media 61, 64, 65
student outcomes 15, 21, 22, 32, 43, 44, 51,
61, 64, 66

Taliban 70, 71
time 13, 23, 32, 33, 43, 53, 55, 85
TLR 35, 64, 75
Tudor, H 21, 23

Upper Pay Scale 23, 75

values 2, 4, 10, 11, 14, 24, 50, 54, 55, 56, 64,
84, 85

WomenEd 3, 15, 17, 81
workload 14, 43, 52, 62

Yousafzai, M 4, 70–77